Masterpieces in the
PITTI PALACE
museums

BELVEDER CON PITTI

206 Colour illustrations

NEW EDITION

BONECHI EDIZIONI ·IL TURISMO· - FIRENZE

Texts by:

Caterina Chiarelli: Historical notes, Boboli Gardens, The Silver Museum, The Costume Gallery, The Carriage Museum, The Porcelain Museum.
Silvestra Bietoletti: The Gallery of Modern Art.
Enrico Colle: The Royal Apartments - The Winter Apartments.
Elisabetta Tenducci: The Palatine Gallery.

© Copyright 1994 by Bonechi Edizioni "Il Turismo" S.r.l.
© Copyright 1997 by Bonechi Edizioni "Il Turismo" S.r.l.
Via dei Rustici, 5 -50122 Florence
Tel. +39 (055) 239.82.24 - Fax +39 (055) 21.63.66
E-Mail address: barbara @ bonechi.com
All rights reserved
Printed in Italy

Translation: Julia Weiss
Photos: Bonechi Edizioni "Il Turismo" S.r.l. Archives
Photos: Rabatti y Domingie: pages 5 -11 - 13 - 14 - 15 - 16 - 17 -
        18 - 19 - 20 - 21 - 22 - 23 - 24 - 25 - 30 - 33 - 41 - 46 - 50 - 57 - 65 -
        67 - 70 - 72 - 73 - 75 - 79 - 81 - 82 - 84 - 86 - 90 - 91 - 96 - 97 - 99 -
        100 - 101 - 102 - 103 - 104 - 105 - 106 - 107 - 108 - 109 - 110 - 111 -
        112 - 113 - 114 - 116 - 117 - 118 - 132 - 133 - 134 - 135 - 136 - 137
        - 138 - 139 - 140 - 141
        Solaria Fotografia: pages 119 - 121 - 130 - 131
        Marcello Bertoni: pages 31 - 34
        Foto Quattrone: pages 35 - 123 - 124 - 125 - 126 - 127 -
        128 - 129
Layout, graphics and cover design: Piero Bonechi
Project coordination and editing: Barbara Bonechi
Type setting: Leadercomp, Florence
Reproductions: La Fotolitografia, Florence
Printing: BO.BA.DO.MA, Florence
ISBN 88-7204-103-1

The Pitti Palace.

THE PITTI PALACE AND BOBOLI GARDENS (Historical Notes)

The Pitti Palace stands on the left bank of the Arno River at the foot of the Boboli hill. Giorgio Vasari (1511-1574) tells us that it was built in the mid-fifteenth century for Luca di Buonaccorso Pitti, a Florentine banker who had commissioned Filippo Brunelleschi to design it while Luca Fancelli, a pupil of the great architect, finished the work. The building fits beautifully into the context of Renaissance palaces and fulfills the requirements of proportion and harmony between the individual parts and the whole. The original design which called for three doors and seven windows on the façade was practically cubic. The only ornamental elements on the rusticated stone (obtained from the quarry on the Boboli hill) façade are the greystone balconies that mark the stories, and the arches around the doors and windows. The unfinished palace was purchased by the Grand Duke Cosimo I de' Medici and his wife, Eleonora di Toledo, in 1550 and work was immediately begun to transform it into their new residence. Bartolomeo Ammannati was appointed to supervise the construction: the first change he made was to design the two huge "kneeling windows", and then he began building the monumental courtyard behind the palace. Again the main material was rusticated stone,

which creates a vibrant "chiaroscuro" effect in alternating bands on the upper stories and combines classic elements such as the three architectural orders, Doric, Ionic and Corinthian with a Manneristic taste for the grandiose. From the first floor the courtyard unfolds like a stage setting towards the Boboli gardens. The original fountain by Ammannati was removed in 1635 and was replaced, sometime between 1642 and 1646, by Franceso Susini's Artichoke Fountain, which is still there today.

In 1565, during the reign of Cosimo I, Vasari the architect of the Uffizi designed and built the long corridor connecting the Uffizi to the Medici family's new home, crossing the Ponte Vecchio and ending north of the Palace alongside of the Grotta del Buontalenti. This architectural feat, now known as the Vasari Corridor was built in just a few months. The family was able to move around safely, shielded from watchful eyes and could control strategic points in the city from a high vantage point. About thirty years later (1590-1595) Bernardo Buontalenti built the Forte di Belvedere under orders from the Grand Duke Ferdinando I on the hilltop to the northeast to protect the palace and gardens below.

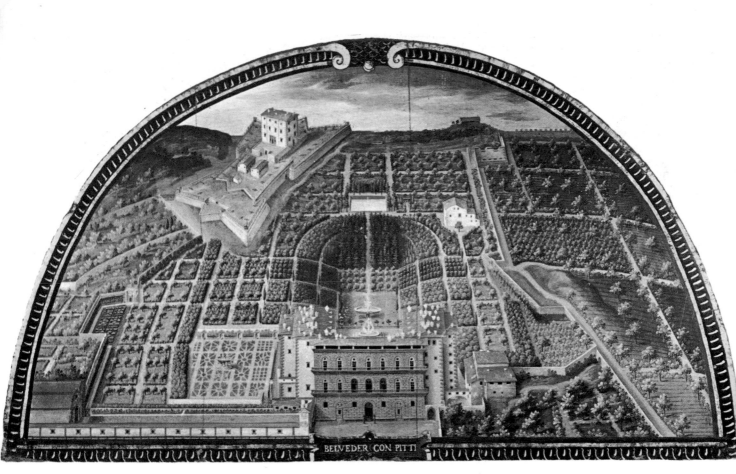

The Pitti Palace and Boboli Gardens, by *Justus Utens* (Museo di Firenze com'era).

Subsequent expansion work also involved the main body of the palace: three windows, designed by Giulio Parigi, were added to each side around 1620 and about twenty years later his son, Alfonso, enlarged the façade to its current size, albeit only on the ground and first floors. The two structures, known as "rondòs" that come toward the square were built under Lorraine rule by the architects Giuseppe Ruggeri (southern rondo, begun in 1764) and Gaspare Maria Paoletti (northern rondo, begun in 1784) and were completed during the reign of Ferdinand III. Later additions did not change the palace's original appearance: architects were already well aware of its historic and artistic value and took care in order that later work would not deviate too harshly from Brunelleschi's original core. Gaspare Maria Paoletti and Pasquale Poccianti designed the Palazzina della Meridiana. This charming building at the southern end of the complex, parallel to the garden, was built between 1776 and 1840. At the northern end of the palace Luigi Del Moro built the atrium and monumental stairs in 1896 that join the summer residence, the piano nobile and the garden.

In 1635 when he married Vittoria della Rovere, the Grand Duke Ferdinando II launched a complex project for decorating the Summer Apartments on the ground floor and the Winter Apartments on the piano nobile, including the recently built rooms. Giovanni da San Giovanni began working on the frescoes dedicated to the celebration of Lorenzo the Magnificent in the first room on the ground floor. However, he never finished the paintings and work was continued by his pupils Ottavio Vannini, Cecco Bravo and Francesco Furini; then the Bolognese artists, Angelo Michele Colonna and Giovacchino Mitelli experts in perspective painting and Pietro Berrettini da Cortona, one of the greatest painters from the Roman Baroque school were summoned to Florence. The artists from Bologna frescoed the three new front rooms on the ground floor, while Berrettini began work on the piano nobile in the Sala della Stufa where he depicted the "Four Ages of Man" (1637-1641). The next six state rooms were completed by his pupil Ciro Ferri. Pietro da Cortona's lavish decorations on the ceilings, dedicated to the planets (represented by ancient mythological gods) were totally innovative with respect to Florentine tradition and provided an example for Baroque painting in the city and other parts of the palace itself.

In parallel with the transformation of the building into a royal residence, Cosimo I ordered Niccolò Tribolo (who died the following year) to build the gardens. The oldest nucleus of the garden began on the slopes of the hill, with bastions built by Cosimo to defend the "Oltrarno" (left bank of the Arno River). Shrubs, bushes and all types of plants, rare and wild, were put in, greenhouses and fountains built in a great fervor of ideas that made Boboli one of the most important Italian gardens in history and literally fit for a prince, if not a king.

One of the earliest projects is the "Grotticina di Madama", at the northern end of Boboli, on the side of Santa Felicita built between 1553 and 1555 by order of Eleonora di Toledo. Its style is similar to the grotto Tribolo designed at Castello, in the Mannerist style of recreating natural environments, populated by mysterious stone animals and creatures. The fountain with the statue of the dwarf Morgante, known as the "Bacchus Fountain" by Valerio Cioli dates from 1560; it is located near the entrance to this part of the garden. It

Right: **The Empire** by *Domenico Pieratti;* below: *Bartolomeo Ammannati's* courtyard.

5

The Artichoke Fountain by *Francesco Susini;* left: the "Bacchus" Fountain by *Valerio Cioli*.

was under the direction of Bartolomeo Ammannati, between 1560 and 1569, that the amphitheater which is perfectly aligned with the palace was built. In 1569 Ammannati was succeeded by Bernardo Buontalenti; his title was "engineer of the gardens" and he also designed the complex at Pratolino for Ferdinando I. Buontalenti created the Grotto (1583-1593) that was built in place of a greenhouse designed by Vasari: the entrance loggia was right up against the exit from the Vasari Corridor and was used as the façade. This grotto, with its strong "scenic" effects bears witness to the architect's creative genius. It is one of the most significant examples of sophisticated and intellectual Florentine Mannerism under the heading of caprice and metamorphosis. Inside we can see casts of Michelangelo's "Prisoners", certainly not admired for their dramatic effects but paradoxically interpreted as exuberant metamorphoses of form. The grotto consists of three chambers in line that were decorated using a wide variety of materials to which water gave color and life: from stalactites and rocks to sponges, shells and terracotta reliefs. The first large chamber is populated by human and animal forms, perhaps representing the

Bernardo Buontalenti's "Grotta", a detail of the façade; right: the "Grotta".

myth of the metamorphosis of Deucalion and Pyrrha, and the ceiling is decorated with frescoes of exotic animals by Bernardino Poccetti. A complex plumbing system made water trickle down the walls, changing the color of the stone and watering the maidenhair ferns. The second room, containing statues of Helen and Theseus by Vincenzo de'Rossi leads into the third with the statue of Venus and satyrs by Giambologna. The room, which is frescoed like a garden, is traversed by a terracotta frieze on which grotesque masks alternate with nymphs.

The other parts of the garden also developed and evolved. Stoldo Lorenzi's statue of Neptune was moved to the center of the fountain sometime after 1576. Higher up, the statue of Abundance, begun by Giambologna and completed by Pietro Tacca was placed against the bastions in 1636. Giulio Parigi transformed the amphitheater into a work of solid masonry in 1631. Between the end of the eighteenth and the middle of the nineteenth centuries, the Egyptian obelisk from Luxor (which arrived in Florence via the Medici collections in Rome) and the basin from the Baths at Caracalla were also placed in the gardens.

The Amphitheatre in the Boboli Gardens; below: the Neptune Fountain.

Under the Grand Dukes Cosimo II and Ferdinando II the garden was enlarged by Giulio and Alfonso Parigi so that on the south side, parallel to the palace, it reached from the hillside to Porta Romana, within the city's walls. The axis is created by the central walk known as the "Viottolone". Alfonso Parigi designed an eliptical pond, with a central island "Isolotto", populated by imaginary and mythological creatures. Giambologna's monumental statue of Oceanus was placed in the middle of the Isolotto. The whole complex is extremely impressive and the effects can be truly appreciated when walking down the Viottolone which is intersected by paths, hedges and statues. The garden is full of ancient statues, stone animals and cheerful modern sculptures (XVII-XIX centuries). During the second half of the eighteenth century the first restorations were launched under Pietro Leopoldo. Works were commissioned that were to last into the following century, done by architects who also worked on the palace itself, such

Right: the "Viottolone"; below: the "Isolotto" with *Giambologna's* Fountain of Oceanus (or Neptune).

Above, from the left: **Playing Civetta,** copy of the original, *XVII century Tuscan School,* and the **Fountain of the Grape Harvest** by *Valerio Cioli;* below: the Limonaia.

Kaffehaus.

as Gaspare Maria Paoletti, Giuseppe Cacialli and Pasquale Poccianti.

Pietro Leopoldo commissioned Zanobi Del Rosso to design two units that were essential to the completion of the gardens, and exemplified rational, enlightened culture: the Caffeehaus and the Limonaia. The first is an elegant open pavilion at the top of a small garden on the hill, a compulsory stop for royal strolls, like in all eighteenth century gardens. The Limonaia, adjacent to the buildings on Via Romana, was built on the site of an old menagerie that housed exotic animals.

Some other important work included the final designs of the gardens in front of the Meridiana, the "Prato delle Colonne" that runs toward Porta Romana and the typical eighteenth century shape of the Neptune Pool.

Over the centuries, certain parts of the Boboli Gardens were dedicated to various celebrations in keeping with a tradition dating from the Medici period; part of that tradition (theatrical performances) had been kept up until recently.

Today, the Pitti Palace houses *The Silver Museum* on the ground floor, the *Palatine Gallery* and the *Monumental Apartments* on the first floor, the *Gallery of Modern Art* and the *Apartment of the Duchess of Aosta* on the second floor, the *Costume Gallery* in the Palazzina della Meridiana, the *Carriage Museum* in the rondò to the right and the *Porcelain Museum* in the Casino del Cavaliere.

Lorenzo the Magnificent with the Artists, by *Ottaviano Vannini* (Room of Giovanni da San Giovanni).

THE SILVER MUSEUM

The Silver Museum is located in the left wing of the Palace, in the former summer apartments of the Medici grand dukes. Today it contains what is left of the Medici treasure, that is, the precious objects and curiosities that were part of the grand dukes' "Wunderkammer". After years in the Uffizi, the Lorraine rulers had most of the items moved to Palazzo Vecchio and then, in the mid-nineteenth century it was decided to transfer the silver, the main part of the Salzburg and Würzburg treasures that Ferdinando III of Lorraine had brought to Florence, to the "Sala di Giovanni da San Giovanni" on the ground floor of the Pitti Palace. And this was the birth of the Silver Museum.

The Medici collections that later found their way into the museum, starting from the nineteen-twenties include semi-precious stone and valuable metal vases, ivory carvings and amber, Florentine inlay tables and furniture, exotic objets d'art and the jewels of Anna Maria Luisa, Palatine Elector and last of the Medici.

Beyond the vestibule, the former entrance room, is the "Sala di Giovanni da San Giovanni" and the **Courtyard of Fame or of Ajax.** In the courtyard (which is usually closed to the public) there is a loggia with three arches, decorated with early seventeenth century grotesques;

the ancient statuary here includes two Roman sarcophagi and *Menelaus and Patrocles*, (formerly believed to be Ajax and Patrocles) a Roman copy of the Greek original.

The *Sala di Giovanni da San Giovanni (room IV)* was the most lavish of all the rooms. It bears the name of the artist who began work on the decorations and frecoes in 1634 which were finished by his pupils between 1636 and 1642. It is the first of the rooms overlooking the façade and was used for court receptions and celebrations.

The frescoes were commissioned for the marriage of Ferdinando II and Vittoria della Rovere (1635). The nuptials are celebrated in an allegorical scene on the ceiling in which Juno and Venus, flanking the Medici coat of arms, surmounted by the grand ducal crown, watch as cherubs raise branches which the Fate Atropos had cut from the thread of life that had been transformed into an oak. Oak, in fact, was the symbol of the Della Rovere family and the branches allude to Vittoria, the last heir. On the walls, *Scenes from the life of Lorenzo the Magnificent*, with allegories related to his life and activities as a patron of arts, with loggias in perspective set against a background of the Tuscan countryside. On the entrance wall, frescoed by Giovanni da San Giovanni, we can see the Satyrs destroying symbols of culture and banishing the Muses from Parnassus. The Muses ask Tuscany for asylum, she is seated above the door and acts as the intermediary for Lorenzo the Magnificent. Lorenzo, on the left, painted by Cecco Bravo, welcomes them. In the middle of the wall facing the entrance, in the fresco by Ottavio Vannini, Lorenzo is surrounded by artists and we can recognize Michelangelo and Giuliano da Sangallo. And finally, on the right side, Lorenzo is shown among the members of the Platonic Academy. In the last scene the Fates cut the thread of life and a swan saves a medal with his portrait from the waters of the Lethe. These frescoes were done by Francesco Furini. Against the entrance wall stands an organ made by Lorenzo Testa in 1703, probably ordered by Ferdinando for the palace, and now recently restored.

From the "Sala di Giovanni da San Giovanni" it was once possible to enter the apartments of the grand duke and duchess on the right and left, respectively. Changes were made in the Sala della Grotticina in the early nineteenth century to make room for Pasquale Poccianti's monumental atrium.

Room II is reached by the door on the left wall and had once served as the *Grand Duchess's audience room*. Today, it contains items *predating the Medici principality*, including 16 semi-precious stone vases that had

Right: **The Muses Banished from Parnassus,** by *Giovanni da San Giovanni;* below, from the left: **detail of the frescoes** by *Vannini* and *Furini,* and of the frescoes by *Colonna* and *Mitelli* in the Grand Duke's Audience Room (Room VI).

Detail of the frescoes by *Angelo Michele Colonna* and *Agostino Mitelli,* Grand Duke's Private Audience Room (Room VII).

belonged to Lorenzo the Magnificent with the initials LAU.R.MED., in the center cabinet. They are made of onyx, jasper, amethyst and sardonyx which, in the XV century were embellished with gilded silver mounts made by Florentine goldsmiths.

Some of the vases that may have belonged to Piero the Gouty when the Medici were banished from Florence, were transferred from the Medici Palace to the Roman residence of Cardinal Giovanni de' Medici, the future Pope Leo X. Pope Clement VII transformed them into reliquaries and as such sent them to the Church of San Lorenzo in Florence to be kept in the tribune designed by Michelangelo. From there they were moved to the Uffizi in 1785 where some of the splendid mountings were removed. And finally, in the nineteen twenties they were brought to the Silver Museum along with the XVI century vases and gemstones. The riches of the original mountings can be deduced from the sixteenth century drawings in the National Library (Cod. Palatino C.B. 3.27). Each one is precious and unique. Just a few of the noteworthy pieces carved from different stones: a Sassanian sardonyx pitcher (Inv.777) with a fifteenth century vermeil mounting and a Medici crest; the middle

vase, from the imperial period, also made of sardonyx (Inv. 507) with a mounting that was remade in the late nineteenth century; two, fourteenth century jasper vases (Inv. 638 and 772) from the Venetian workshops with mounts added by Florentine craftsmen in the following century; two pairs of bowls (Inv. 804, 685) in amethyst quartz, one of which still has its original XV century mount and Medici emblem. And immediately behind the vases we can see the *Portrait of Lorenzo the Magnificent* from the school of Bronzino.

In the two lateral displays we can see mainly Roman and Byzantine vases and bowls from the Medici collections, some of which were already inventoried in Lorenzo's day. Note the Roman (I cent.A.D.) sardonyx "simpulum" for libations; a rock crystal vase from the Fatimide dynasty (1000-1009); two small chalcedony bowls from the I century A.D. with enameled gold mounts made in the grand duke's workshops in the last quarter of the XVI century; and finally a small porphyry Venus and Cupid by Pier Maria Serbaldi of Pescia (1455-1515) an artist who gave new meaning to the art of semi-precious stone engraving and reintroduced it to Italy.

Detail of the frescoes by *Angelo Michele Colonna* and *Agostino Mitelli* in the Grand Duke's Private Audience Room.

The central display on the right contains fabrics that were restored at the "Laboratorio di Restauro Tessili" of the Costume Gallery. Currently (1993) we can see vestments from the Vallombrosa Monastery dating from the late XV century: a cope, a chasuble and two tunicles in rich fabric with appliqued embroideries. In the two display cases on the walls, there are reliquaries and goblets from the XIV and XV centuries including an "encolpion" that is a pendant reliquary to be worn on the neck, in the shape of a cross in an oval inlaid with precious stones (late fourteenth century German), a triptych depicting the Passion and Crucifixion in Limoges enamel dating from the early XVI century by an artist from the school of Pénicaud, whose initials were "M.P.".

The next room (*III*), known as the *"grotticina"* with its seventeenth century fountain, is where the grand duchesses had their hair done; it led to the bedroom and the mezzanine and the Wardrobe, which were all altered by Poccianti's designs. Other "casualties" in the rebuilding were Filippo Tarchiani's decorations (1630 ca) that covered the walls and most of the ceiling which was also repainted. The marble floor was repaired with

sixteenth century panels sometime during the nineteen thirties. Today the room contains portraits of the grand duchesses: *Johanna of Austria* by Giovanni Bizzelli, *Vittoria della Rovere* by Justus Sustermans, *Christine of Lorraine* by Scipione Pulzone, *Maria Magdalena of Austria* by Sustermans and *Marguerite-Louise d'Orléans* by an unknown painter. On the left wall, a complex wooden relief sculpture depicts the *allegory of the arts and friendship among princes* with a medallion-portrait of Pietro da Cortona by Grinling Gibbons in the middle, a gift of Charles II of England to Cosimo III (1682). The marble putti on the walls date from the XVI-XVII centuries and some are supposedly Roman copies of ancient Greek works.

Going back through the Sala di Giovanni da San Giovanni we can enter the **chapel** frescoed in the style of Matteo Rosselli in the early seventeenth century. Here we can see the Medici silver made by Florentine craftsmen in the XVII century and, near the altar, the processional cross from Salzburg (XVII cent.).

Beyond the chapel we find ourselves in the *apartment of the grand duke* and the *three reception rooms* frescoed by the Bolognese artists Angelo Michele Colon-

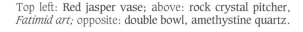

Top left: **Red jasper vase**; above: rock crystal pitcher, *Fatimid art;* opposite: **double bowl, amethystine quartz.**

na and Agostino Mitelli, masters of perspective painting, up to then a specialty of that area. The two artists were summoned to Florence in 1636 upon the death of Giovanni da San Giovanni and they completed the work in 1641.

The first room (*VI*) is the *grand duke's audience room*, with a monumental painted circular staircase and majestic telamons in the foreground that support a balcony; the entire upper part of the room is circled by a false balcony beyond which we can see various genre scenes such as a child hiding behind a railing trying to catch a monkey. On the ceiling an *Allegory of Strength, Justice and Time* by Colonna, and in the middle of the room stands the inlaid ebony cabinet with semi-precious stone mosaic and painted panels. The central compartment contains a four-sided revolving altar: amber figurines are on two sides, an in-laid panel on the third, and on the fourth a painting of the Virgin and Child. In the top part there is a small organ that was once connected to a clock and it played on the hour. This masterpiece was made in Augsburg for Philip Hainhofer, a German merchant.

The Archduke Leopoldo bought it as a gift for his brother-in-law, Ferdinando II on the occasion of the

Double bowl carved from jasper.

Early XVII century German cabinet.

latter's visit to Innsbruck in 1628. The drawers contained precious gems.

The ebony and semi-precious stone prie-dieu was made for Ferdinando II in the grand-ducal workshop. The upper portion contains a mosaic of the *Baptism of Christ* by the Roman artist Giovanni Battista Calandra (1610-20) based on a painting by Santi di Tito that had belonged to Cosimo II. The mosaic replaced a painting of St. Mary Magdalene which, in the inventories had been attributed to Leonardo da Vinci.

The next room (*VII*) was the *private audience room*, decorated with a perspective painting of a colonnade. The ceiling frescoes show Alexander the Great in a chariot among the clouds, and over the doors the coats of arms of Ferdinando II and Vittoria della Rovere. "Beyond" the columns there are more genre scenes: a child playing with a parrot and another looking out the window onto the square. These effects, however, are no less impressive than the ceiling: on either side of the door that led to the grand duke's bedroom, a double staircase that a court official seems to be climbing, and a large edicola in the foreground with a scene from the life of Alexander the Great; and the perspective architecture seems to extend far beyond. Against the walls there are Florentine mosaic tables made in the grand-ducal workshops in the late sixteenth century. Here, and elsewhere in the museum there are several types of

inlaid table tops, ranging from the simplest to the most complex floral patterns. One of the most significant is the chessboard made in 1609 to a design by Jacopo Ligozzi; it is set into porphyry, decorated with flowers and butterflies, in keeping with the naturalistic style of his works.

The last room in the group (*VIII*) was the *third audience room*, which via the atrium and staircase designed by Luigi del Moro in 1896 leads to the garden and the Palatine Gallery. On the ceiling *Jupiter Descends from Olympus to Give the Symbols of Power to the Medici*, was frescoed by Colonna, and the walls, with their majestic architectural frescoes were done by Mitelli. The two doors led to the servants' quarters.

The table, an ancient porphyry *rota* with three sleeping marble putti in the middle belonged to Cosimo I. Between the two doors is a fine cabinet made in the grand-ducal workshops to drawings by Giovambattista Foggini (1709), who was the master of the shops under Cosimo III. It is made of ebony with semi-precious stone relief work panels that were partially replaced in the XIX century by flat inlays, and gilded bronze ornaments. It was a gift from Cosimo III to his daughter Anna Maria Ludovica, when she lived in Düsseldorf as wife of Johann Wilhelm von der Pfalz, the Palatine Elector. She brought it back to Florence when her husband died in 1717. In the central niche, topped by the Medici-Pfalz coat of arms, is the portrait, carved in semi-precious

Detail of the frescoes by *Angelo Michele Colonna* and *Agostino Mitelli* in the Third Audience Room (Room VIII).

stone, of the Elector, behind the two little side doors there are two groups of gilded bronze putti.

Another noteworthy piece is the small reliquary in the shape of a temple with statues of Dominican saints that was also made by Foggini (1713). The semi-precious stone figures were carved in the early seventeenth century by Francesco Mocchi and by other artists up to 1705. The *Deposition between the Virgin and Angels*, is a wax model by Massimiliano Soldani Benzi, goldsmith and sculptor who worked for both Cosimo III and Ferdinando. The piece comes from the Montalve Convent.

The oval table with the wooden base in the shape of harpies leaning on volutes and separated by a vase has been identified as the table that was once in the bedroom of Cosimo I, and has been attributed to the carver Dionigi Nigetti (1574 ca).

On the side opposite the façade were the *grand duke's private apartments*. The ceilings are lower because of the mezzanine above, and they are not frescoed, though according to the inventories, in the XVII century, they were well furnished and decorated with many framed paintings. Today it contains the treasure of the grand dukes that was brought from the Uffizi. The room where the grand duke "bathed" (*IX*) contains mainly *seventeenth century ivories* carved by German and Flemish masters; this collection was started by Cardinal Leopoldo in the XVII century.

Right: turned ivory vase from Coburg; below: Casket by *Valerio Belli.*

Lapislazuli cup by *Giovambattista Cervi;* left: gallery table fountain from the Sarachi workshop.

There is an unusual story behind the collection of 27 ivory vases that were brilliantly executed by Marcus Heiden and his pupil Johann Eisenberg for Johann Casimir, duke of Coburg between 1618 and 1631. The duke himself was an amateur turner and had collected the vases in his palace at Ehrenburg from where they were taken when the imperial troops besieged Coburg (September, 1632) during the Thirty Years' War. The young Prince Mattia de' Medici fought with the Imperial army and received them as booty which he sent to his brother, the Grand Duke Ferdinando II. Entrance wall, on the right: here we can works by two German artists, Philipp Sengher and Balthasar Permoser. Sengher, an ivory carver who probably came from Augsburg worked at the grand ducal court from 1675 to 1704 under both Cosimo III and Ferdinando. He made two ivory medallions with a *Portrait of Cosimo III* and his initials which are joined by a chain and were both carved from a single block of ivory. Sengher also made the two vases in Eisenberg's style. And there is an interesting story: after he had taught his art to Ferdinando, as we can see from the vase (Inv. Bargello n.45) he made, Cosimo III sent the master to work for Peter the Great in

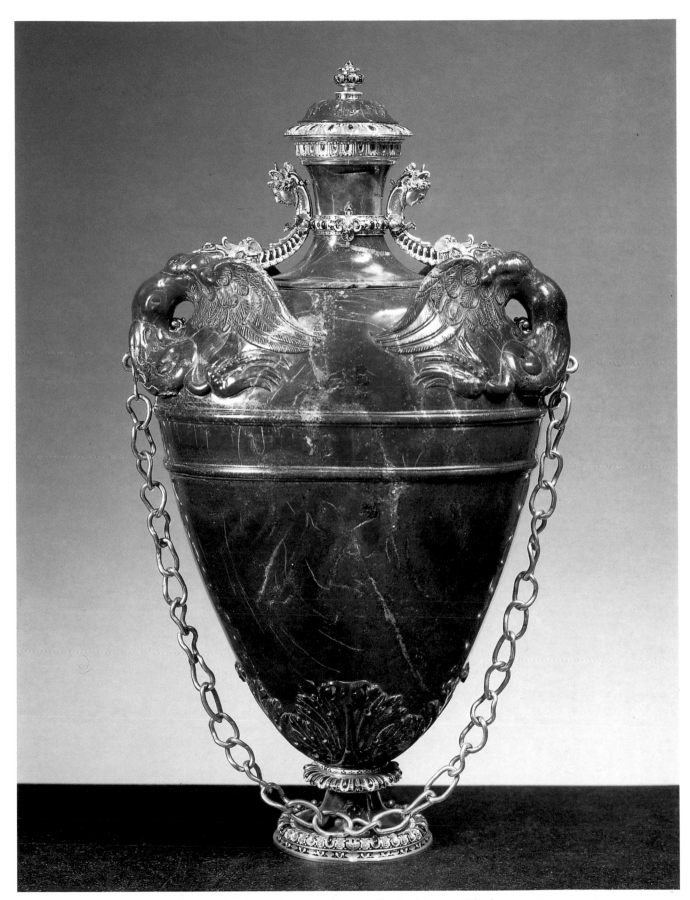

Lapislazuli vase by *Bernardo Buontalenti* and *Jacques Bilivelt*.

Gold and semi-precious stone inlay by *Bernardino Gaffuri* and *Jacques Bilivelt.*

Russia. To thank him, the Tzar sent the grand duke the ivory compass (Inv. Bargello n.40) and a Ko-ssu hanging (see room XX). Balthasar Permoser was a sculptor who worked in Florence from 1676 to 1690. He carved the *Portrait of Violante of Bavaria* and presented it to Ferdinando on the occasion of his marriage to the German princess in 1689.

Many of the ivories in the showcase to the left of the door belonged to Cardinal Leopoldo's collection, including a series of putti and reliefs in the style of the Flemish sculptor François Duquesnoy (who worked in Rome from 1618 to 1643). The statue of *Curtius Flinging Himself into the Abyss* is by a German artist known as the Master of the Furies and dates from the mid XVII century.

The inlaid wood table and cabinet with floral motifs are by the Dutch cabinet-maker Leonard van der Vinne, known as "Tarsia". During the years he worked for the grand dukes (1659-1713) he brought this new fashion of marquetry to Florence, with its floral patterns and many tulips. The two pieces, made in 1664 and 1666 respec-

tively were immediately recognized as works of art and were taken to the Uffizi. But although the artist remained in Florence, the technique did not enjoy any great development.

Room X, ivories and reliquaries. To the right of the entrance: a globe with an ebony support with miniature portraits in ivory of *Wilhelm V, Duke of Bavaria and His Family* by Giovanni Antonio Maggiore (1582) of Milan, one of the first great ivory carvers. The globe, which Francesco I received from the Duke of Bavaria and placed in the Tribune was part of the tradition of princely gift-giving that developed in that period. Note the caged horse carved from a single piece of ivory by Filippo Planzone of Sicily who worked in Genoa and gave it as a gift to Ferdinando II (1624), and the ebony box topped by an ivory dog that had belonged to the Grand Duchess Maria Magdalena.

The other two display cases contain items by German sculptors who worked in Italy for many years such as Permoser and Balthasar Stockamer. The latter came from Nuremberg. He studied in Rome, a protégé of

Gold bas-relief sculpture on amethyst base from the Grand Duke's workshops depicting "The Endeavors of Francesco I".

Cardinal Leopoldo, and stayed at the Villa Medici (1664-1669) where he copied ancient works and the work of Pietro da Cortona. Fine examples of his work are the small ivory figurines based on classic subjects such as *Bacchus, Venus and Cupid*, and *Apollo* that were probably copied from ancient statues at the villa. *Hercules and the Hydra*, among the classic subjects and *The Seated David and The Crucifixion*, from the religious subjects (both on the left wall) reveal a greater maturity in his art.

Only few reliquaries remain of the once rich collection in the palace chapel: part was sent to San Lorenzo in 1785 in exchange for semi-precious stone vases and many were destroyed by the French army in 1799. Note the gilded silver reliquary with semi-precious stones for the Holy Cross, perhaps made by the goldsmith Cosimo Merlini. It was probably made in the grand-ducal workshops in the late seventeenth or early eighteenth century as a companion piece to the other reliquary of the cross which is next to it, using a French made mirror for the central portion. The casket of the Holy Se-

pulchre, made of gilded silver, gemstones and gold reliefs on a lapis lazuli background dates from the era of Gian Gastone.

Beyond the room leading to the stairway, where we can see the bronze relief *Crucifixion* by Giovambattista Foggini (1677) we enter *room XI, or amber room and formerly the grand duke's bedroom*. Above the door is a framed tapestry portraying *Cosimo III* by the Medici court weavers (made prior to 1676). On the opposite wall is a painting attributed to the "so-called" Marcuola depicting *Gian Gastone receiving the young Cosimo Riccardi* in this very same room.

There are three cabinets that Cosimo III had ordered built between 1726 and 1728 to contain the amber and ivory objects from the collections of Maria Magdalena, Cosimo III and the Grand Duke Ferdinando. Maria Magdalena had collected a considerable number of amber pieces in her chapel. This valuable material, much in vogue among royalty, was used for state gifts by the Prussian monarchs, and it is believed that most of the Medici amber all made in Germany is of such origin. Amber is a very fragile resin and only a few pieces have been preserved. Those that remain, dating from the XVI and XVII centuries, form the core of this collection. The most significant item is the the altar in the middle of the large cabinet: the craftsman was Georg Schreiber of Königsberg (1618-1619), a fine sculptor whose medium was amber. He worked for the Brandenburg Elector for many years, making state gifts. The cabinet decorations, with shells and turbaned heads are a reference to the marine and African origins of amber and ivory, respectively. Silver figurines by Giambologna depicting the *Labors of Hercules* decorated the two smaller cabinets, and a large uncut emerald atop the larger one were all taken by the French in 1799. An amber table-fountain from Germany is the most important non-religious item in the collection.

On the right hand wall we can see a semi-precious stone portrait of *Vittoria della Rovere* by Giuseppe Antonio Torricelli (1662-1719) from the Montalve Convent. It is believed to have been commissioned by Cosimo III in 1694 upon his mother's death, and was completed in 1713; it is considered the first life-size portrait in semi-precious stones. An inlaid table, made from semi-precious stones in the imperial workshops in Prague under Rudolph II stands on a gilded wood base made by the Dutch carver Victor Crosten (1704). A painting of *Saint Anne with the Virgin* by Francesco Solimena (early XVIII century) in a frame with silver flowers which belonged to the Palatine Elector and a silver

Cameo of Cosimo I, by *Giovanni Antonio de' Rossi*.

relief, *The Deposition*, from XVIII century Rome are the other important items in the room.

Room XII, formerly the privy council now houses the collection of *XVI and XVII century rock crystal and semi-precious stone vases*. It is one of the most impressive rooms with those sumptuous items that were once kept in the cabinets built into the Tribune and probably never used to decorate the grand dukes' tables. The oldest vases were made by Milanese stone carvers such as Sarachi and Miseroni in the second half of the sixteenth century. But soon craftsmen from Milan brought their skills to the Florentine workshops of the grand dukes at the Casino di San Marco. Francesco I summoned Ambrogio and Stefano Caroni to Florence in 1572 and in 1575 they were joined by Giorgio di Cristofano Gaffuri. Then came the goldsmiths who made the rich mounts for the vases only part of which have survived. These masters included Hans Domes from Flanders (who worked in Florence from 1563 to 1601), the Dutchman Jacques Bilivelt who arrived in 1573 and worked with Buontalenti and finally Eduard Vallet, from France who came in 1588. Vases and bowls in strange manneristic shapes, shells, fish and sea monsters and symbolic scenes in relief but mainly richly engraved abounded. The Milanese artisans were most adept at vases in the shape of animals, dragons, birds and fish. The Sarachis specialized in galley vases. It is worthwile noting the fine gold or gilded silver mounts made for the vases, embellished with enamel, cameos, gems and such minute patterns that they cannot even be seen from a normal viewing distance.

In each cabinet there are pairs of rock crystal and agate columns made by Bernardino and Cristofano Gaffuri for the unfinished ciborium of the Chapel of the Princes. The eight semi-precious stone statues of saints (some made to designs by Orazio Mochi at the beginning of the seventeenth century) are also from the chapel.

The shelves holding the vases were originally in the gem room in the Uffizi (1782). Starting from the right: vase carved from a single piece of rock crystal, unengraved, with a gold mount by Eduard Vallet 1618). Right wall: a Hydra-shaped vase surmounted by Hercules, probably from the Sarachi's workshop (latter half of the XVI cent.); shell-cup on a dolphin by Giovambattista Metellino of Milan (late XVI, early VII century). Opposite wall: engraved rock crystal triumphal column, Milanese workshop, mid sixteenth century).

The cabinets on the left wall and near the door contain many pieces that Catherine de'Medici had bequeathed to her granddaughter Christine of Lorraine and which came to Florence when she married Ferdinando I in 1589. The most important pieces in this group include the casket by Valerio Belli of Vicenza (1530-32) one of the first engravers of semi-precious stones. The casket is made of gilded and enameled silver, with scenes from *The Passion* engraved into the rock crystal and silver on the back. It is one of the greatest glyptic masterpieces of the early sixteenth century. Both the overall structure and the style were inspired by classic Renaissance culture. It was a gift from Pope Clement VII to Francis I, king of France when his second son, the future Henry II married Pope Clement's niece, Catherine de'Medici in 1533. Noteworthy too is the rock crystal and gilded silver plate with engravings of Noah's Ark, attributed to

Bust of Augustus by *Antonio Gentili da Faenza,* the head is antique turquoise and the torso is made of gold.

Giovanni dei Bernardi di Castelbolognese (1546) who, after Valerio Belli, was the greatest carver of rock crystal in the first half of the sixteenth century. The Gasparo Miseroni bowl (ca 1559) was made for the same event, with its fine French style, pierced and enameled lid on which we can see the initials "H C" for Henry and Catherine that have ambiguously been read as "H D" referring to Diane de Poitiers his mistress. Yet another fine piece is the rock crystal amphora with the reclining Venus from the Sarachi workshop (late XVI century) and an hexagonal rock crystal flask with transverse enameled gold bands from the same workshop. The galley table fountain by the Sarachis with scenes from the life of Noah and a lid in the shape of a sea monster was also a wedding gift. One of the most famous pieces in the entire museum is the majestic lapis lazuli vase made in the grand ducal workshops to designs by Bernardo Buontalenti, architect to Francesco I, in 1583, with an enameled gold mount by Jacques

Rooster pendant, *XVI Flemish workshop*.

Bilivelt. In the same showcase there is a snail-shaped lapis lazuli cup with an enamelled gold snake handle by the Florentine goldsmith Giovambattista Cervi (1576). It is typical of the items from the grand ducal workshops with their clean, naturalistic lines. In the center of the room stands a semi-precious stone table that had belonged to Cardinal Ferdinando and had been in the Villa Medici in Rome (dated prior to 1587).

We reach the *mezzanine* via the secret staircase that once led to all the floors. It was blocked off in the early XIX century when Elisa Baciocchi had a bathroom built on the Piano Nobile to prepare for the arrival of her brother, Napoleon I. The mezzanine contained the private treasure of the grand duke who held the only keys.

Room XIV, the cameo room. Collecting cameos, intaglio and signet rings was long a Medici tradition. Piero the Gouty's inventory already listed a large number; Lorenzo the Magnificent was a passionate collector and the grand dukes, expanded and organized the collection which was divided between the Archeological Museum and the Silver Museum in the XIX century when it was removed from the Uffizi.

The center display case contains: the onyx cameo of *Cosimo I* one of the largest from the Renaissance, *portraying the grand duke, his wife Eleonora and four children* by Giovanni Antonio de'Rossi (1557-1562). Vasari tells that us originally it was even bigger and there was a medal of "Fiorenza" in the now empty center. Next come the seven gold bas-reliefs made from wax models by Giambologna, on semi-precious stone bases depicting the *Endeavours of Francesco I de' Medici*. Then there is an oval with a bas-relief in gold on semi-precious stones of *Piazza Signoria* with an equestrian statue of Cosimo I in the foreground by Jacques Bilivelt (who did the bas-relief in 1600) and Bernardino Gaffuri (background 1599). The seven bas-reliefs made for the central temple of the Uffizi designed by Buontalenti for Francesco I were placed in the cabinet ordered by Ferdinando I who also ordered the oval. Other

The Knife Sharpener, *German-made, late XVII century.*

Mermaid pendant, *Flemish-made, XVI century.*

sixteenth century imitation of exotic objects, worthy of a "Wunderkammer": perhaps the oak branches allude to the patron, Vittoria della Rovere. A minute mosaic picture by Marcello Provenzale (1615) with birds, a gift of Cardinal Scipione Borghese to the Medici (1632): this particular mosaic technique using tiny pieces, and therefore, so different from the Florentine inlays, developed in Rome and Provenzale became one of its foremost practitioners.

Room XV, the room of the jewels, is dedicated mainly to the "bejewelled *galantries*" of the last Medici, Anna Maria Ludovica. As Palatine Elector she was very aware of all the latest novelties that came to Germany, so that many of these precious curiosities were made in Northern Europe. Unfortunately, the "trinkets" in the showcases are only part of the collection that the widowed Anna Maria brought back to Florence and kept in a cabinet in her apartment in the Pitti Palace. Upon her death, Francis Stephen of Lorraine sold off, not only the crown jewels, but also the most valuable items in this collection to obtain funds for his bankrupt coffers. What remained of her jewels was moved to Vienna in 1750: a small part was taken to the Hofburg along with the treasure of the Austrian Emperors and was returned to Florence in 1923 after the Treaty of St. Germain. The main focus of these "bejewelled *galantries*" is the baroque pearl, each one is different and each one inspired the creation of natural or imaginary figures embellishing the central pearl with lively and complex fittings made of the finest materials: gold, gems and enamel. They were made by German, Flemish and Dutch craftsmen in the sixteenth and seventeenth centuries. Among the pendants we can see several subjects: two gondolas, more or less realistic animals such as a splendid dragon and a majestic rooster; mythological characters such as a fierce triton and a crowned mermaid clutching an hourglass and sceptre with the sun on one side and moon on the other. Then there are the animal knick-knacks: some such as the cow, ostrich and peacock are very life-like. A group of bizzare and grotesque figurines made in Germany in the late XVI early XVII centuries includes a soldier and a cobbler. Ivory statues trimmed with gold, semi-precious and gemstones and enamel are late seventeenth century German, but can be traced to the court goldsmiths. The most intricate ones are a knife-sharpener and two similar groups with a mule-driver leading a mule with a monkey on its back. Then there are nine unusual buttons made of enamelled gold, pearls and gemstones depicting soldiers, made by Flemish artists in the late sixteenth century. A piece by the goldsmith Peter Boy the Elder in engraved and enameled gold holds the arms of the Medici-Pfalz electors (1708-1724). And finally a group of small items made of valuable materials, including baroque pearls, ivory and semi-precious stones, and near her jewels, a portrait of the Electress by Anton Domenico Gabbiani.

On the left wall is an ex-voto of *Cosimo II*, showing *the grand duke kneeling at an altar*, in inlaid mosaic, gold, gems and enamel. It was meant for the altar in the Church of St Carlo Borromeo in Milan, but Cosimo died of illness before it was completed. It remained in Florence and the gold frontal was melted down in 1780. The display case contains rings with semi-precious

noteworthy cameos include the portraits of the Medici family members along with some jewels found in the family's tombs in San Lorenzo such as the rock crystal, enameled gold and topaz cross of Cardinal Carlo de'Medici. The cameos with historical or mythological subjects include the *triumphal entry* attributed to Domenico Romano (latter half of the sixteenth century).

Along the walls are small busts with ancient heads of emperors, perhaps used at command bastions or imperial court ceremonies. One of them, an antique turquoise head of *Augustus* on a gold bust was made by Antonio Gentili of Faenza (1580) for the future Grand Duke Ferdinando I. The cases on the left wall contain a series of small semi-precious stone perfume jars and busts of classical inspiration from the XVI and XVII centuries, brought from the Tribune. The other items include the symbolically complex seal of Cosimo I, a plasma intaglio by Domenico di Polo (1532) depicting Hercules, ancient symbol of the Florentine Republic with a gilded silver handle with Lorenzo's three rings and feathers and on the base a scroll with the Medici arms and the grand ducal crown. A turquoise mask framed by gold leaves decorated with enamel and diamonds is a strange

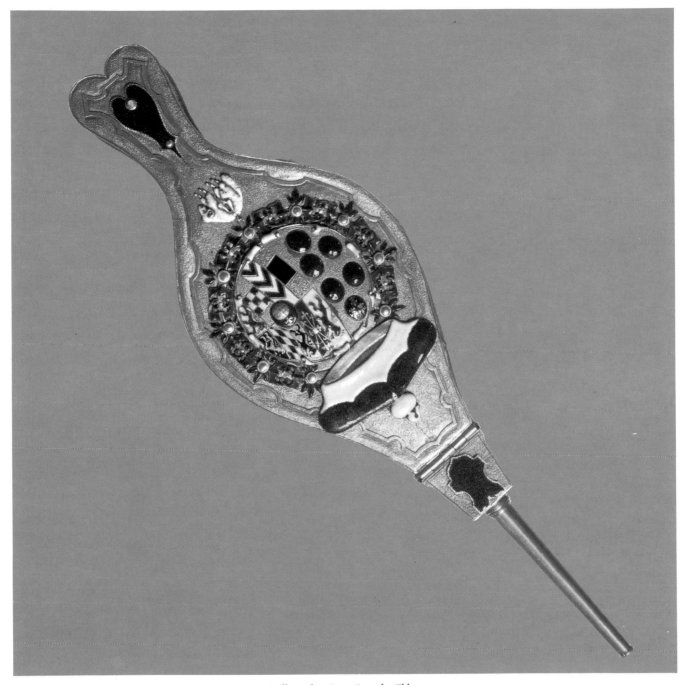

Bellows by *Peter Boy the Elder*.

stone intaglios and cameos, while the case on the right wall has other intaglios including the famous cornelian with the profile of Frà Girolamo Savonarola made by Giovanni delle Corniole between 1498 and 1516.

Left of the stairs in *rooms XVI and XVII* we can see ceilings decorated by Florentine painters in the XVII century, during the reign of Ferdinando II and Vittoria della Rovere. The first ceiling, attributed to Cecco Bravo, portrays *Prudence, Fame and Justice*, while the second one, most probably the work of Ottavio Vannini, has an octagonal panel of *The Coronation of Juno* surrounded by putti in niches, playing with the "balls" from the Medici arms. These two rooms contain the *treasure of Ferdinand III of Lorraine*, acquired during his exile in Vienna. He had fled to the safety of his

brother's court (Francis I, Emperor of Austria) when French troops invaded Tuscany in 1799. In 1801 his brother granted him the principality of Salzburg when it was secularized and the prince-bishop deposed, and in 1805 he was also granted the principality of Würzburg. When he returned to Florence in 1814 he brought much of the bishops' treasures including tableware and furnishings from the chapel of the Renaissance prince-bishop Wolf Dietrich von Raitenau (1587-1612).

Room XVI: on the right stands a display case containing church silver, including a container for holy water from Salzburg made of partly gilded silver by Abraham Pflegel of Augsburg (1577). Among the items from the chapel of the Archbishop Wolf Dietrich von Raitenau of Salzburg (from the right) we can see: a gold *Crucifixion*

St. Michael, *made in Vienna, late XVII-early XVIII century.*

In the middle of the room we can see the travel altar: a finely crafted and complex piece made of valuable materials: gilded silver with figures and decorations in alabaster, tortoise shell, mother-of-pearl, coral, agate, plasma and gemstones. The crucifixion scene on top is made of alabaster, while the scenes from the Passion below are coral. The lack of any hallmarks, and the fine crafting have led experts to believe that it was made for some royal court; it was part of the 1753 Salzburg inventory.

Room XVII contains the lavish, gold plated silver dinner service that had belonged to the archbishop Wolf Dietrich von Raitenau, made by Augsburg goldsmiths around 1585-90 and purchased by the prince's agents during the Diet of Regensburg. Starting from the right: two pitchers and bowls in gilded, embossed and hammered silver; the dishes used as fingerbowls are decorated with scenes of Orpheus and animals enchanted by his lyre and bear the hallmarks of Cornelius Erb (who made them between 1580 and 1585) and Paul Hübner (made from 1585-1590). The fifty-four sweetmeat bowls, grouped by size and subject are truly a unique set. From the left, the first six show the *theological virtues* and *seasons* by Cornelius Erb; they are followed by 36 pieces made by Paul Hübner showing the *elements, virtues, the months* and *twelves scenes from the life of Jacob* and then twelve smaller ones, again by Hübner, with *the elements* and the *virtues*. Although

Dragon pendant, *made by Flemish craftsman, XVI century.*

attributed to Paul Van Vianen, a Dutch goldsmith (ca 1600); a set of silver cross and candlesticks late XVI and early XVII century, respectively (southern Germany); engraved silver altarpiece depicting the *Madonna and Child*, surrounded by sixteen panels with *Scenes from the Life of the Virgin Mary*. The center scene on the altarpiece is based on a painting by Kaspar Memberger, official painter of the archbishop's court, while the smaller scenes were inspired by Giovanni Stradano's prints (1590 ca).

On the right wall a showcase is dedicated to an interesting and mixed group of XIV and XV century drinking cups made of horn, ostrich eggs, veined wood and shells with gilded silver mounts. Many are "double cups", or rather ewers with the smaller of the two used as a chalice. These closed containers were used to prevent the bishops' drinks from being poisoned as they were brought to table. Two German-made Gothic style horn drinking cups from the Salzburg treasure are exceptionally noteworthy. The oldest one (1370-1380 ca) is supported by a knight and the second (1400-1420 ca) rests on an eagle that symbolizes Christ. There is also an unusual cup made from a seashell on a sixteenth century mount that still reflects some Gothic influence.

these allegories are clearly Northern in style, especially the backgrounds and landscapes, we can see the Italian Renaissance influence in the figures.

Three of the four cups with harpy-shaped handles are from the collection of Wolf Dietrich von Raitenau (the fourth is decorated with the arms of his successor Marcus Sitticus von Hohenems, bishop from 1612 to 1619), as is the gold-enameled flask by Hans Karl of Nuremberg, goldsmith to the archbishop's court who signed and dated it (1602).

The complex scenes on two cups depict episodes from the life in the gold mines near Salzburg; in fact, they were a gift to the prince-bishop from the mining company. The same display case also contains a gilded silver dolphin-shaped pitcher (probably from Augsburg, 1609) whose companion bowl has been lost; engraved steinbock horn cups, and silver figurines of the twelve emperors from a seventeenth century German astronomical clock. Of the "household" items that had belonged to Ferdinand III, such as the bedwarmers from Würzburg, bells and wicklamps, the pièce de resistance is his travel case. It's an early nineteenth leather-covered box containing nearly everything from toilet articles to breakfast dishes made in workshops throughout Europe including Paris, and (these date from 1769-1789) each piece is marked with Ferdinand's "F" and coronet.

The subdued, neoclassic vermeil dinner service made by the Parisian goldsmith Martin-Guillaume Biennais (1764-1843) who worked for the imperial court was designed by Charles Percier. This, along with other silver by Biennais had belonged to Elisa Baciocchi who had ordered it from Paris in 1809. Her 1814 attempt to take the silver to France failed and when Ferdinand III gained possession of the items he had his cypher engraved on it; later the House of Savoy replaced that with their own coat of arms. The same showcase also contains two gilded silver pitchers and bowls from Augsburg made in the late XVI-early XVII century and as well as two large silver vases (1700 ca) of the same provenance.

We now go through a closed *loggia (XVIII)* that once opened onto the Courtyard of Fame, which is decorated with early seventeenth century frescoes of grotesques and panels depicting the crafts and discoveries of new civilizations. The lunettes above the doors are decorated with paintings of caged birds and exotic animals (1624-36). Below the detail of the fresco depicting the *Discovery of America* there is a painting on canvas by an anonymous seventeenth century artist portraying the life-size figure of *Montezuma*, the last King of the Aztecs. And it is this "exotic" note that leads us into *room XIX* dedicated to *items made overseas*.

The frescoes in this and the adjacent room, which both open onto the courtyard loggia where trompe l'oeil bowers and birds, broken by landscapes and allegories, allude to cool outdoor settings much like a nymphaeum. Many of the items in these rooms meet the criteria of "Wunderkammer curiosities" and still display some scientific interest in distant civilizations; from the right: three ivory horns from West Africa, actually used to summon the people. Two of them are richly engraved with patterns typical of the Congo area in the sixteenth century. We don't know whether they were gifts or

Austrian altarpiece, *late XVI-early XVII century.*

acquired by the Medici's agents in Portugal. The examples of Moghul art from Jaipur include a seventeenth century mother-of-pearl box and a nephrite cup with a setting by French craftsmen made of gold and diamonds, presented to Ferdinando II by the Elector of Saxony around 1554. There is a fine group of engraved nautilus shells from China with elaborate mounts that came to Europe in the XVI and XVII centuries including a gilded silver pitcher with gemstones that had belonged to Francis I and a gilded silver cup. Both items are made of nautilus shells and the mounts are from XVI century Flemish workshops. German-made items from the next century include a gilded bronze saltcellar, surmounted by Neptune with two seahorses as supports, and a vase with a strange gilded bronze and silver mount consisting of a figure in exotic costume, a seahorse and a putto riding a snail. Also from China are the rhinoceros horn cups and some rare antique porcelain: a plate and two Celadon pitchers from the XIV century. The plate was presented to Lorenzo the Magnificent by the Bey of Egypt in 1487. There is also a blue and white Ming vase (early XVI century) the only piece that remains of the huge Medici collection of Chinese porcelain that was sold off after the death of the last grand duke in 1737. This vase was copied in an inlay panel made by the Opificio delle Pietre Dure at the end of the XVIII century; it can be seen in the Pitti Palace Tapestry Collection.

The display on the left wall contains grotesques and bizzare busts and statuettes in the style of Arcimboldo. Made of shells on papier-mâché bases, they date from around 1600 and were supposed to decorate the small grottoes that were once built into the palace's rooms.

Small loggia decorated with frescoes, *early XVII century.*

To the left of the entrance we can see the Mexican items such as anthropomorphic or animal-shaped amulets, and a jade votive or funerary mask from the V-VI century Teotihuacan tradition. There is also a fine mitre with a Mexican colonial (1520-1547) feather mosaic infula in pre-Columbian technique. The subjects: *The Passion and Crucifixion* show a clear native influence in many of the details. By 1586 this item was already in Rome in the "wardrobe" of Cardinal Ferdinando and then Ferdinando I.

Room XX, Chinese porcelains: these items were not in the Medici collections, they belonged, instead to the Duchy of Parma and were collected by the Bourbons and Marie Louise second wife of Napoleon Bonaparte and duchess of Parma, Piacenza and Guastalla from

1816 to 1831 and passed on to Savoy ownership in 1860. In 1864-65 when the Savoys moved to the Pitti Palace in Florence they brought all the collections, practically stripping bare the palaces of the former duchy. The "blanc de Chine", white and blue, pink and green XVIII century sets of Chinese porcelain all come from Parma, while the small, XVII century mountain-shaped groups were part of the Medici collections. On the walls we can see valuable fragments of seventeenth century Chinese decorative fabrics for chairs and tables used for official ceremonies. The fine Ko-ssu piece was a gift to Cosimo III from the Russian Tzar (1711) along with the ivory compass displayed on the floor below. After having been kept in warehouses for decades it was cut up in 1842 to make drapes for the lunette in the

Flask, *made in the Netherlands, mid XVI century.*

Fragment of a Chinese ceremonial tapestry, K'O-ssu technique; opposite page: Early XX century English necklace.

Chinese room, and then restored and put on exhibit in 1981.

Room XXI, Japanese porcelain. The ceiling frescoes date more or less from the same period as the decorations in the other rooms. The eighteenth century Japanese Arita porcelain and the Chinese items made in the Japanese style in the XVIII century are all from the Parma collections while the Japanese lacquerware pieces (seventeenth century) based on western shapes were already in the Medici collections by the XVIII century.

Room XXII, new acquisitions: these recent donations of gold, enamel and gemstones dating from the seventeenth century to the nineteen thirties were made in Europe and Italy. One of the oldest items is a seventeenth century corset pin. The colored enamel and gemstones set into the corollas make the floral motif highly realistic. There is also a good selection of naturalistic-floral jewels where the gems outsparkle the settings: this style originated in the XVIII century and made a comeback in the early XIX: several pins, crowns and sets were made in France during this period. There are also elaborate contemporary sets in which the gold prevails leaving little room for either enamel or stones. There is a noteworthy group of Sicilian jewels distinguished by the "baroque" styling that favors bright colors, much enamel, stones and pearls. The many necklaces and earrings cover a long period since one of the most important items, a necklace, dates from the XVII century. The nineteenth century Neapolitan corals, including a mermaid-shaped bracelet, a floral necklace, and parasol fittings are strong evidence of Romantic tendencies in the Risorgimento that gave a strong impetus to typically Italian crafts such as coral carving at Torre del Greco. Still in the Romantic context, the archeological revival is evident in the small pictures and miniature Roman mosaics depicting famous monuments and mythological subjects set in frames and held together by tiny chains. Nor is there a lack of Etruscan-style jewels such as the filigreed pin and earrings in the style of the Castellani family's goldsmiths who launched the fashion or of jewels inspired by Egyptian art. The use of turquoise, frequent in English jewels with pavé settings was also related to the revival of interest in Egyptian art. Also typical of the English romantic style are the love tokens such as the pin dated 1801 with a lock of hair. There is fine group of déco jewels, including an articulated snake necklace with enamel and various types of bracelets, rings and earrings. There is an excellent collection of small watches: the gold cases are decorated with enamel, gems and pearls; the shapes range from apples and pears to shells, musical instruments and globes. There are also several types of boxes and seals, made of various materials dating from different periods. The center display case contains some particularly significant items: a pectoral cross with "tremblant" from the eighteenth century consisting of small baroque pearls that form vines contrasted by another in diamonds from the belle époque; a mid-nineteenth century French floral set made of diamonds and pearls; a gold and enamel belt from the mid-nineteenth century; a platinum tiara with amethysts and diamonds by Cartier; an early XX century choker with diamonds, emeralds and sapphires, of greatly understated elegance from England.

On the right side there is a showcase with other bequests including an interesting collection of XIX century pocket watches and silver such as the Biennais teaset Napoleon used during his exile on St. Helena.

Room XXIII and the corridor of the casts (XXIV): there are 58 plaster casts of large dishes on the walls. Every year Cosimo III and his male heirs received one on the Feast of St. John by bequest of Cardinal Lazzaro Pallavicini of Genoa. These signs of gratitude were made in Rome and depict *scenes from the lives of the Medici* with special emphasis on the last members of the family. The tradition which began in 1680 ended in 1737 with the death of Gian Gastone, and the original silver was melted down by the French in 1799. All that remains are the casts made in the mid-eighteenth century for the Doccia porcelain factory and donated to the museum by the Marchese Leonardo Ginori Lisci. And they are indeed fine evidence of Roman sculpture and silversmithing over two centuries.

The church silver from the XVII and XVIII centuries in this room was brought to Florence by the Bourbons in 1801 when they were made Kings of Etruria by Napoleon, and by the Savoys. The pieces come from the ducal palaces in Parma: the most important items are the silver lectern, a group of eighteenth century goblets, pitcher and bowl, all from different workshlops.

Room XXV and the corridor of the silverware (XXVI) on the walls we can see paper and colored wax reliefs in the style of Gaetano Zumbo from the XVII century. The cupboard in the hallway contains the few pieces of church silver left after the palace chapel was looted by French troops in 1799. Note the ostensorium with the Lorraine coat of arms, hallmarked by Gaetano Guadagni, made after 1815; the statuettes come from the lavish reliquary of the patron saints of Tuscany which Cosimo III commissioned Giovambattista Foggini to make for the chapel of the relics in 1718. The statues were hidden in the wardrobe, while the reliquary was melted down by the French. Then there are two mother-of-pearl inlaid wood models from the church of the Holy Sepulchre in Jerusalem and the Basilica of the Nativity in Bethlehem, dated 1699; and altar-cards from the XVII and XVIII centuries. On the walls, the terracottas by Massimiliano Soldani Benzi (1711) depict *Allegories of the Four Seasons* and they were used as models for the bronze reliefs which, today, can be seen in the Bayerisches Museum in Munich (Germany). The Grand Duke Ferdinando had presented them to his brother-in-law, the Palatine Elector.

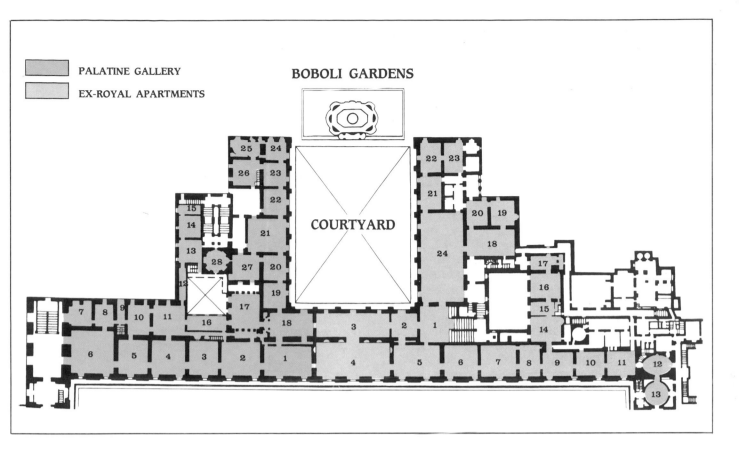

PALATINE GALLERY

1 – Venus Room. 2 – Apollo Room. 3 – Mars Room. 4 – Jupiter Room. 5 – Saturn Room. 6 – Iliad Room. 7 – Stove Room. 8 – Room of the Education of Jupiter. 9 – Little Bathroom. 10 – Ulysses Room. 11 – Prometheus Room. 12 – Corridor of the Columns. 13 – Justice Room. 14 – Flora Room. 15 – Room of the Putti or Cherubs. 16 – Poccetti Gallery. 17 – Music Room. 18 – Castagnoli Room. 19 – Allegory Room. 20 – Room of the Fine Arts. 21 – Hercules Room. 22 – Aurora Room. 23 – Berenice Room. 24 – Psyche Room. 25 – Vestibule and Bathroom of Maria Louise. 26 – Fame Room. 27 – Room of the Ark. 28 – Chapel of the Reliquaries.

EX-ROYAL APARTMENTS

1 – Vestibule. 2 – Antichamber of the Footmen. 3 – Hall of the Statues. 4 – Niches Room. 5 – Green Room. 6 – Throne Room. 7 – Blue Room. 8 – Chapel. 9 – Parrot Room. 10 – Yellow Room. 11 – Bed Chamber. 12 – Queen's Dressing Room. 13 – Queen's Study and Sewing Room. 14 – Bed Chamber. 15 – Royal Study. 16 – Reception Room. 17 – Antichamber. 18 – Bona Room. 19 – Temperance Room. 20 – Prudence Room. 21 – Faith Room. 22 – Charity Room. 23 – Justice Room. 24 – White Ballroom.

THE PALATINE GALLERY

Introduction

Of the many art collections housed in the Pitti Palace, the Palatine Gallery is definitely the most important. The Gallery, situated on the piano nobile is famous for its XV to XVIII century masterpieces (enhanced by their sumptuous frames, many of which date from the seventeenth century) and the opulence of the rooms themselves which were once the winter quarters of the grand dukes (the former summer quarters are now the Silver Museum), the rooms overlooking the front (known as the "rooms of the planets", frescoed by Pietro da Cortona) and the private rooms in the back. The histories of the Gallery and its paintings are closely linked to the Medici family's active patronage of the arts and the fact that they had chosen the Pitti Palace as

their private residence in the mid-sixteenth century. As we shall see further on, the building was home to members of the Medici family until 1737, that means the grand dukes and their many relations, including Cardinal Leopoldo (1613-1675) and Cardinal Giovan Carlo or the Grand Duke Ferdinando (1663-1713) heir to the throne who died young. They decorated their suites with many artworks which are now displayed in the Gallery. Their collections, destined solely for private enjoyment (the Gallery par excellence and hence the official one was always the Uffizi) through the last will and testament of Anna Maria Luisa (1743) last of the Medici line, became the inalienable property of the city along with the remaining works, and was further

enriched by the acquisitions of the Hapsburg-Lorraine dynasty, Grand Dukes of Tuscany from 1737 to 1848. Therefore, the Palatine Gallery, as we more or less know it today dates from the Hapsburg-Lorraine rule: the grand dukes gathered the artworks that were scattered throughout the Pitti Palace and various Medici homes and villas that were often abandoned or even partially destroyed. It was Peter Leopold of Lorraine, who began putting some of the paintings that were still in the Gallery into the rooms frescoed by Cortona and decorated with tapestries on the walls, (used mainly to ward off the winter cold). He did not change the private character of the apartments which also include bedrooms in the front. Some of the first paintings to be moved, the *Portrait of Leo X* by Raphael (now in the Uffizi) and the *Four Philosphers by Rubens* were put in the Mars Room, while Raphael's *Madonna of the Chair* was moved to the Jupiter Room. Actually it was Ferdinand III and Leopoldo II who were responsible for the more decisive arrangement of the Palace's "picture gallery" (hence the name Palatine – of the palace). The criteria they followed from the end of the XVIII century were not organic, but exquisitely decorative and had already shaped the tastes of their predecessor Peter Leopold. Notwithstanding subsequent shifts and rearrangements, the Gallery still maintains the same atmosphere. It was opened to a select public in 1833 (the first printed catalogue dates from 1828) and today we can see it as the richest and most splendid example of a private "picture gallery" in any royal residence.

Giangastone de' Medici, by *F.M. Richter*; below: bronze bust of Cosimo I de' Medici, by *B. Bandinelli* (Grooms' Antechamber).

The Grooms' Antechamber
The Room of the Statues
The Room of the Niches

The entrance to the Palatine Gallery proper and the wing known as the Quartiere del Volterrano is preceded by a few separate rooms: the Grooms' Antechamber, once part of the loggia that overlooked the inside courtyard; the Room of the Statues and the Room of the Niches. They were decorated by Giuseppe Castagnoli (Florence, 1754-1832) and Giuseppe Maria Terreni who worked on the Room of the Niches, during the era of Ferdinand III of Lorraine (1791). The Room of the Statues contains several important seventeenth century paintings: the oldest of these is *The Dentist*, attributed to Caravaggio (Michelangelo Merisi b. 1571, Caravaggio-d.1610, Porto Ercole). Authorship was confirmed by recent (1991) X-ray examinations. Painted during the last part of his career, the canvas has been in Florence since 1637. The subject, a genre scene is shown by forcing the expression of feeling in favor of marked realism through the use of light which makes the painting something of a prototype of a style that would become quite common among Merisi's followers. Pieter Paul Rubens (b.1577, Siegen-d.1640 Antwerp) painted the *Christ Resurrected* around 1616 and it was added to Prince Ferdinando's collection in 1713. The painting, an unusual portrayal of the Resurrection, was

Ceiling frescoes by *Pietro da Cortona* in the Venus Room.

still markedly influenced by Italian painting (especially the Venetian school and Annibale Carracci) due to the artist's long sojourn in Italy (1600-1608).

The Rooms of the Planets

The decorations in the front rooms were commissioned by the Grand Duke Ferdinando II and were done by Pietro Berrettini, also known as Pietro da Cortona (b.1596, Cortona-d. 1669, Rome). He worked in Florence in 1637 and 1640 (when he painted the frescoes in the "Sala della Stufa" see below) and from 1641-1647. During that period he worked on the Rooms of the Planets which, however, were completed by his pupil Ciro Ferri (b. Rome 1634-d.1689) from 1659-1661 and 1663-1665. In the rooms dedicated to the planets, perhaps in honor of Galileo Galilei, a protégé of the Medicis, on the basis of subjects suggested by the Grand Duke's librarian, Francesco Rondinelli we can see the Ptolemaic hierarchy of the heavens, even though the Moon and Mercury are not represented. The first room, in fact is dedicated to Venus and the others, in order, to Apollo, Mars, Jupiter and Saturn. Two figures are constant in all the ceiling frescoes: the prince (the future Cosimo III who succeeded his father Ferdinando II

in 1670) and Hercules, recognizable by his club and lionskin, symbol of the prince's virtues and depicted practically as his tutor and companion on the road to power. The young prince will be taken from the arms of Venus (and that is from flattery and the pleasures of love) to be educated in the arts and letters of which he, like the god Apollo, will be patron, and then on to become a brave warrior tutored by Mars; Jupiter will crown him and Saturn, in the apotheosis will welcome him to Olympus.

His contemporaries already considered Cortona's frescoes one of the greatest examples of Baroque emphasis on enhancing the reigning family through triumphal allegories and clear metaphors inspired by myth, history and religion. These goals were pursued through elaborate and "marvelous" settings that certainly astounded (and indeed that was their purpose) those who waited in the rooms to be received by the grand duke. The ceilings, are infinite spaces containing luminous skies in which the lightness and liveliness of the figures is created by the clear colors based on warm pinks and reds, greens and gilded yellows accenting the soft flesh of the figures that are interwoven with the turgid white and gilded plaster figures on the sides (designed by Cortona and executed under his supervision.

The Venus Room: *Antonio Canova's* statue of Venus Italica is in the middle.

The Venus Room

This first room was created from two smaller ones, the wardrobe and vestibule of the grand duke's apartments after the fire of 25 October 1638 prompted the architect Alfonso Parigi to convince Ferdinando II to build one large room. This was the first antechamber in which "all types of persons" waited to be received in the throne Room (that is, the Jupiter Room): a small grating between the plaster reliefs that can still be seen looking up and to the left with one's back to the window, made it possible to see what was happening inside.

The goddess, Venus, to whom the room is dedicated is depicted in the ceiling frescoes: the young prince is torn from her arms by Minerva, goddess of wisdom and patron of the arts, to be taken to Hercules. The lunettes on the walls portray famous characters from antiquity (Cyrus, Alexander, Antiochus, Antiochus III, Scipione, Augustus and Crispus) as examples of moderation. The white stucco ovals show the two Medici popes (Leo X and Clement VII) and the grand dukes from Cosimo I to Cosimo III as a child.

In the middle of the room, in homage to the goddess is the *Venus Italica*, sculpted by Canova in 1810. This statue was made to replace the *Medici Venus* that the French requisitioned from the Uffizi Tribune in 1799 and took to the Louvre along with many other Florentine artworks.

After 1815 and the fall of Napoleon the statue was returned to its original setting and Canova's Venus was moved to the Pitti Palace.

The walls are hung with great masterpieces. On the right is one of Titian's (b.1490?, Pieve di Cadore-d.1576 Venice) most famous paintings, *Portrait of Pietro Aretino*, the man of letters from Arezzo who lived in Venice from 1527 and was a great friend of the painter. The character's unusual and unsettling spirit is skillfully conveyed with great immediacy. It is free of flattery and reflects classic sculptures that embodied Aretino's ideals: the man was educated in Rome. He commissioned the painting in 1545 and sent it to Cosimo I de' Medici as a gift in the same year saying that "it (the painting) breathes, pulsates and moves the spirit in the same manner as I do in life."

Titian also painted the *Portrait of a Lady ("La Bella")*. It was dubbed with that title when, at the end of the eighteenth century in an attempt to identify the model, a certain resemblence to the *"Venere di Urbino"* in the Uffizi was noted; it was believed that the woman in both portraits had been Titian's mistress. Mentioned for the first time in a letter dated 1536 from Francesco Maria, Duke of Urbino to Titian, *"La Bella"*, with her charming face, deep bosom and beautiful blue brocade dress, with soft white puffs on the sleeves, came to Florence along with the bequest of the Grand Duchess Vittoria della Rovere (1631).

The other paintings by Titian are *The Concert* and the *Portrait of Pope Julius II*. The first painting was purchased by Cardinal Leopoldo de' Medici in Venice in 1654 and placed in the Tribune and then in the Pitti Palace from 1697 on as part of Prince Ferdinando's collection. Originally it had been attributed to Giorgione and is now recognized as having been painted by the young Titian (c 1510). Of the three people in the painting, which today's critics tend to identify with three musicians – the "concert" theme was very popular in Italian fifteenth and sixteenth century cultured circles – an older tradition, oddly enough, had identified them as Calvin, Martin Luther and the former nun, Catherina von Bore whom Luther married in 1525. It is more appropriate to suppose that the musical theme is related to the "three ages of man", the theme of Giorgione's painting in the Jupiter Room: music acquires an important and essential value in "every phase of civilized life."

The *Portrait of Pope Julius II* is a copy of the famous painting by Raphael, originally made for the Church of Santa Maria del Popolo in Rome and now in the National Gallery in London. Probably painted for the Grand Duchess of Urbino around 1545 and sent to Florence with the Della Rovere bequest, Titian's painting while a faithful copy does indeed transform the model. The execution is typically Venetian: clothing and face are filled with light, and the character's psychology seems centered in the penetrating and haughty gaze.

Another important Venetian painting is the *Portrait of Baccio Valori* by Sebastiano del Piombo, (Sebastiano Luciani b.1485 ca, Venice-d. 1547, Rome). It was painted sometime after 1530 and mentioned by Vasari in his *Lives*. An important fact about the painting which effectively grasps the model's expression is that it was one of the first works done on slate, a technique which, over the years has led to evident changes in the dark colors.

Seventeenth century art is well represented in this room and the next. The most famous paintings from this period are the two canvases by Pieter Paul Rubens, *Ulysses on the Island of the Phaeacians* and *The Peasants Return from the Fields*, dating from around 1630-1635. They were both in the Duke of Richelieu's collection and probably were sent to the Pitti Palace during the Lorraine period. These are intensely poetic works, with incredible shadings in the luminous green of the landscape, revealing the painter's Baroque penchant for the dramatic effects of weather with masses of clouds and rays of sunshine that illuminate the horizon. Although set in similar contexts the two paintings deal with the subjects in entirely different ways: the *Ulysses* is closer to classic reminiscences (where the architectural details and cart in the background are clearly classic) while the *Peasants Return from the Fields* is more naturalistic. It is likely that Rubens painted it with Lucas van Uden (Antwerp 1595-1672) a renowned landscape painter.

Venus Italica by *Antonio Canova* (Venus Room).

Giovan Francesco Barbieri, known as Guercino (b.1591 Ferrera-d.1666 Bologna) did *The Flaying of Marsyas* in 1618 for Cosimo II, grand duke of Tuscany. The plays of light and shadow that have caused it to be defined as a "romantic vision" are also proof that the painter was acquainted with the works of Giorgione and Titian. *Apollo and Marsyas* by the Florentine painter Giovanni Bilivert (Florence, 1585-1644) is painted in more muted and reserved tones. Bilivert's teacher, Ludovico Cardi, known as Cigoli (b. 1559, Cigoli-d.1613, Rome) painted the large canvas of *Jesus Appears to Peter*. Recently restored and dated around 1607 it is one of the most important examples of the artist's mature work as a founder of Baroque painting in Florence.

The Concert; below: Portrait of Pope Julius II; two paintings by *Titian*. Opposite page: "La Bella" by *Titian*.

Another seventeenth century artist was Salvator Rosa (b.1615, Naples-d.1673, Rome). The Palatine Gallery owns several works by this Neapolitan master: many are in the Psyche Room and depict *Battles, Seascapes* and *Allegorical Scenes* painted for Medici patrons during the artist's Florentine sojourn from 1640-1649. Here, in the Venus Room are two seascapes showing a *Port*, painted for the Medici Cardinal Giovan Carlo and influenced by Claude Lorrain's painting of the Port, done for Ferdinando II in 1638 and the *View of the Lighthouse*.

The Peasants Return from the Fields, by *Pieter Paul Rubens;* below: Seascape by *Salvator Rosa*
(Venus Room).

The Apollo Room; below: Mary Magdalene by *Titian*.

The Apollo Room

"The first antechamber of the nobility", the Apollo Room was decorated by Cortona between 1643-1646, but completed by Ciro Ferri in 1660 to Cortona's drawings. The frescoes show Apollo, god of the arts and sun as the symbol of enlightened power, accompanied by Glory and the Virtues, while Hercules bears the weight of the world. The bases show the Muses and the lunettes contain scenes in which ancient emperors and warriors are shown as protectors of the arts and letters: Augustus listening to a reading of the Aeneid, Alexander the Great and Homer's poems, Justinian and the Pandette and Julius Caesar listening to historical works.

Portrait of a Man, or The Man with Grey Eyes by *Titian*; below: Madonna Enthroned and Saints by *Rosso Fiorentino;* opposite page: Holy Family by *Andrea del Sarto* (Apollo Room).

This room also contains great paintings by Titian. One of the most famous is *Mary Magdalene*, probably painted between 1530 and 1535 for Guidobaldo, duke of Urbino and brought to Florence with the bequest of Vittoria Della Rovere.

This canvas, with one of Titian's most frequent subjects has been recently restored and reveals warm colors in the flesh and the golden veil created by her hair. This painting of incomparable value which emphasizes the subtle sensuality of image is both a prototype of religious devotion and filled with the ambiguity of much Baroque art. Again by Titian the *Portrait of a Man* also known as *The Man with Grey Eyes* or *The Englishman*, an unknown person painted in an informal and modern pose. The arm casually by his side reveals the nobility and charm of his personality as does his penetrating gaze. The monumental image, with its severe greys and blacks is enlivened by the flesh tones and white lace on the collar and cuffs; the clothing and hair make it possible to date the painting around 1540-1545.

Early sixteenth century painting is represented by the *Luco Pietà* and the *Medici Holy Family* by Andrea del Sarto and the altarpiece with the *Madonna Enthroned and Saints* by Rosso Fiorentino. The Del Sarto panel (Florence 1486-1530) purchased by Peter Leopold in 1782 was painted between 1523-1524 for the high altar of the church of San Pietro at Luco in the Mugello where the painter had fled to escape the plague epidemic in Florence. Inspired by the *Lamentation over the Dead Christ* by Fra Bartolomeo, it had been in the Jupiter Room and was recently restored to its original splendor. Andrea del Sarto's use of a different and more "modern" color range and monumental figures reveals that he had learned about Michelangelo's and Raphael's Roman painting. It served as a basis for Florentine Mannerist painters and in particular his pupils Pontormo and Rosso Fiorentino. The *"Medici Holy Family"* and a painting of the *Madonna and Child with St. Elizabeth and St. John* is apparently from his later period. The serene and quietly religious air is a fine example of how devoted feeling influenced Florentine painting during the Counter Reformation.

The altarpiece of the *Madonna Enthroned and Saints* by Rosso Fiorentino (Giovanni Battista di Jacopo, b. 1495, Florence-d.1540, Fontainebleau) was painted for the Dei Chapel in the Church of Santo Spirito. It was removed and replaced by a copy by order of Ferdinando de' Medici in 16901. It was enlarged on all sides so that it could fit into a bigger frame. The additions are especially obvious on the top part of the painting in the niche above the Virgin and Child. The lively colors and many figures create a subtle atmosphere of motion and tension

Finally, we must mention at least one more painting in this room: *The Hospitality of St. Julian* by Cristofano Allori (Florence, 1577-1621), a student of Cigoli and son of Alessandro, one of the leading figures in late sixteenth century Florentine painting. Allori, was one of the major artists of the Florentine Baroque school and there are many of his paintings in the Palatine Gallery. In *The Hospitality of St. Julian*, one of his finest works, Allori depicted an uncommon subject and that is, Jesus in the foreground pardoning Julian who had lived a life of penitence after having inadvertently killed his parents.

The Mars Room; below: detail of the ceiling, Allegory of War by *Pietro da Cortona*.

The Mars Room

In the ceiling frescoes (1645-1647) with the Medici coat of arms in the center, topped by a crown with Ferdinando's name, Cortona celebrated the prince's military virtues. He is portrayed victorious thanks to the god's intervention, in the form of rays, in a sea and land battle along the edges of the ceiling. The scene is most impressive (especially the wave-tossed ships) and reflects contemporary theatrical performances that astounded the royal courts in Rome. The prince's triumph is symbolized by the trophy Hercules creates with the remains of the enemies that the Dioscuri brought him, while Victory flanked by Peace and Abundance is crowned and receives the prisoners. War is also the subject of a famous painting by Rubens which hangs in this room: *The Consequences of War*. It was ordered by Justus Sustermans, the Flemish painter who lived in Florence in 1637. The painting arrived in 1638 and was transferred to the Pitti Palace in 1691 when Ferdinando

The Consequences of War; below: The Four Philosophers, two paintings by *Pieter Paul Rubens*
(Mars Room).

de' Medici purchased it from the deceased painter's
heirs. There was a long letter from Rubens with the
painting explaining the iconography and the painter's
anguish over the difficult situation in Flanders comes
through in the bloody scenario. The Temple of Janus is
opened (it is closed during peace) and Mars throws
himself into the battle although Venus, who is counter--
balanced by the Fury with torch in hand and the two
monsters, plague and hunger, "inseparable compan-
ions of war" tries to stop him. War "which corrupts and
destroys everything" overturns harmony (the woman
on the ground with the broken lute), "fertility" (the
woman holding a child) and civilization (the architect
lying at the far right of the painting: the good that is
done in peace is destroyed by war) while Mars, stamps
on the book and "tramples letters and other fine
things." At the feet of the figure on the left, Europe in
black mourning, lie an olive branch and a caduceus,

Portrait of Cardinal Guido Bentivoglio by *Anton van Dyck;* right: Portrait of Ippolito de' Medici, by *Titian* (Mars Room).

symbols of peace. The tragic violence of the subject is matched by excited and rhythmic tones (almost a march) and it is all emphasized, especially on the right side, by bright colors that contrast with Venus' pale skin.

Rubens also painted the *Four Philosophers* who, from the right are Rubens himself,his brother Philip and the humanists Justus Lipsius and Jan Van de Wouwère; in the background we can see the ruins of the Palatine hill and the Church of St Theodore in Rome. The bust of Seneca in the niche on the right has lent the painting to neostoic interpretations in which courage and the strength of moral virtues combat contemporary corruption. The painting, done around 1611-1612 reveals the influence of Titian's and Tintoretto's Venetian paintings on Flemish art: here they are absorbed and transposed in the warm colors, fast brush strokes and rich subject matter.

Another fine example of seventeenth century Flemish art is the *Portrait of Cardinal Guido Bentivoglio* by Anton van Dyck (b.1599, Antwerp-d.1641 London) which was painted around 1622-1623 and given to Ferdinando II in 1653 by a member of the Bentivoglio family. This painting, which is considered to be one of Van Dyck's masterpieces, launched a new generation in celebrative portraiture. Flemish attention to the naturalistic and elaborate rendering of detail (in the fabrics, books and objects) comes together in this painting with the monumental force of the image and its throbbing reds. The liveliness is also highlighted by the subject's keen eyes; the Cardinal wrote the History of the Wars of Flanders.

Titian painted the *Portrait of Ippolito de' Medici* in Bologna in 1532, that is the year following the expedition against the Turks. Ippolito, illegitimate son of Giuliano, Duke of Nemours, also joined in the expedition, so he is portrayed in Hungarian costume, and yet attention is immediately drawn to his face, its smooth lines and penetrating expression.

Two other masters of sixteenth century Venetian painting Veronese (Paolo Caliari,b. 1528, Verona-d.1588, Venice) and Tintoretto (Jacopo Robusti, Venice 1518-1594) are represented in this room by the *Portrait of a Gentleman* and *Portrait of Luigi Cornaro*, respectively. The first, purchased in Venice in 1659 portrays an unknown model, probably a Venetian nobleman wearing a lynx fur over his plain black clothing. This high quality painting accents the refined elegance of the subject and probably dates from the 1560's. *The Portrait of Luigi Cornaro*, a Venetian man of letters, patron

Portrait of Alvise Cornaro by *Tintoretto;* right: Portrait of a Gentleman by *Veronese* (Mars Room).

and friend of artists, shows him late in life and close to his death which occurred in 1566. The painting was acquired by Cardinal Leopoldo in 1675 and became such a favorite of Ferdinando's that it was hung in the Alcove as early as 1698.

In addition to the famous canvases by Rubens and Van Dyck, other fine examples of seventeenth century painting in the Mars Room are works by Bartolomé Esteban Murillo (Seville, 1618-1682) and by Lodovico Cardi, known as Cigoli.

Murillo was known for the elegance and idealized beauty of his works that were inspired by true devotion and so readily fulfilled the religious needs of seventeenth century Spanish spirituality (nearly all his works were for churches). The Palatine Gallery owns the two paintings in this room: the *Madonna of the Rosary* and the *Madonna and Child* which well illustrate the artist's poetic skill. Both date from Murillo's young period, around 1650. The first reached the Pitti Palace in 1822 when it was bought by Ferdinando III of Lorraine the exact date the second one arrived is unknown even though it is certain that it comes from a convent at Ypres.

Cigoli was one of the key artists of XVII century Florentine painting. The Palatine Gallery has many of his paintings and in this room we can see the *St Mary Magdalene*, his most controversial painting because of the many copies that had been made. The painting has been recently (1992) restored to its original splendor. Dated around 1600, it has been in the Pitti Palace since 1663 and reflects Cigoli's studies on Venetian painting (great naturalistic effects as evidenced by the Crucifix or the skull in the foreground) and introduces the subtly erotic atmosphere that distinguishes many Florentine religious paintings of that period. *The Sacrifice of Abraham* by Cigoli is essential proof of the artist's Roman experience (in the early 1600's along with Annibale Caracci and Caravaggio he was considered one of the foremost painters in Rome). The painting, which was in the Villa del Poggio Imperiale since 1654, was commissioned by Cardinal Arrigoni and done in 1606-1607. Related to prototypes by Andrea del Sarto and Pontormo (and therefore to sixteenth century Florentine artistic traditions) the painting does reveal his knowledge of developments in Roman art, especially Caracci's work and it encompasses the poetry of emotions (in the balance of the composition, the tranquility of the gestures and expressions translated into a painting of softened effects) determining factors in the subsequent development of Florentine painting.

The Jupiter Room with *Vincenzo Consani's* Victory in the center; preceding page: Madonna and Child by *Bartolome Esteban Murillo* (Mars Room).

The Jupiter Room

This room which was once the Throne Room is dedicated to Jupiter, king of the gods. Cortona's frescoes (1643-1646) depict Jupiter, whom we can recognize through his symbols, the eagle and lightning bolt surrounded by the Virtues, as he crowns the prince who has alighted from the Argo with Hercules and Fortune. Behind the prince we can see Victory (engraving a letter M for Medici on a shield), Mars the god of war and Wrath enchained. The lunettes show scenes of peace: Vulcan no longer makes weapons, Apollo causes a rebirth in the love of the arts, Diana does not hunt, Minerva brings the olive tree, Mercury is a herald of peace and Fury enchained vainly invokes discord; the Dioscuri put the horses to rest and Mars leaves the earth riding on Pegasus.

The most famous painting in this room is Raphael's *Portrait of a Woman ("La Velata")* (b. 1483, Urbino-d.1520, Rome). According to Vasari's accounts the woman is Margherita, known as "La Fornarina" daughter of Francesco Luti of Siena and said to have been Raphael's mistress. The rich gowns, painted with incomparable skill, are soft and sumptuous, and mainly

the veil and the hand over her heart would indicate a married woman, even if the painting is very similar to the *"Portrait of the Fornarina"* which is the in the Barberini Palace collection in Rome. This painting came to the Pitti Palace in 1621 as part of the Marchese Matteo Botti's bequest. Up to the end of the last century it was not even recognized as having been painted by the master from Urbino. Today, it is one of Raphael's most famous portraits and approaches his ideal of beauty as expressed in the *Madonna of the Chair* (Saturn Room); *"La Velata"* has been dated around 1516.

Another painting, *The Three Ages of Man* is dated around 1500. Recent restorations (1987) have confirmed that it was indeed the work of the great Venetian painter, Giorgione (b.1477 Castelfranco Veneto-d.1510 Venice). In the past it had been attributed to both Giovanni Bellini and Lorenzo Lotto, it can be identified as one of the paintings that was part of the Vendramin collection in Venice from 1567-1569 and arrived at the Pitti Palace in 1698 when it was purchased by Ferdinando. The monumental power of the three characters

The Three Ages of Man, by *Giorgione*; opposite page: "La Velata" by *Raphael.*

against the dark background shows the influence of Leonardo da Vinci. The subject, though traditionally known as *The Three Ages of Man* is actually a concert scene or singing lesson, a frequent theme in Northern Italian painting between the XV and XVI centuries.

The Pietà, or *Lamentation Over the Dead Christ* by Fra' Bartolomeo Della Porta (b.1472 Prato-d.1516, Florence) dates from the early sixteenth century (1510-1512). The panel is from the monastery of San Gallo which the Florentines had destroyed along with all other monasteries outside the city walls in 1529 to prevent the quartering of the foreign troops who were beseiging the city. The painting was purchased by Cardinal Carlo de'Medici in 1619; since 1531 it had been in the church of San Jocopo tra i Fossi where, due to the proximity of two rivers the painting was often damaged by floods. The mutilation of the painting probably dates from the year of its purchase. The upper part was damaged, perhaps to put it in a smaller frame, more suitable for private devotions and perhaps to modernize it in accordance with Baroque tastes, covering the figures of St Peter and St Paul. Only recent restorations (1985-1988) have returned the painting, albeit irremediably mutilat-

ed, to its original version: a devoutly religious picture which inspired many Florentine artists of the period including Andrea del Sarto. There are two paintings by this master in the Jupiter room: the *Annunciation* also done for the San Gallo monastery and kept in the church of San Jacopo tra i Fossi since 1531. It was brought to the Pitti collection in 1627 by order of Maria Magdalene of Austria, widow of Cosimo II. It is one of the basic works in Andrea's career and although it is still linked to the Florentine tradition of the early 1500's, that is, Filippino Lippi and Fra' Bartolomeo, it reveals his familiarity with contemporary Roman art (Michelangelo and Raphael) thanks to a journey he made around 1511. The painting, in which the classic element is joined by the new tensions, such as the restless figures in the background, also provided the foundations for subsequent developments in the works of Del Sarto and his two pupils, Pontormo and Rosso Fiorentino. *St John the Baptist* dates from Andrea del Sarto's mature years; it was painted for Giovan Maria Benintendi in 1523 and destined, along with other paintings, to decorate an antechamber in his palace. The panel, which Benintendi gave to Cosimo I, shows an unusual portrayal of the

Pietà by *Fra' Bartolomeo Della Porta* (Jupiter Room).

Saint, as a heroic character, taken from classical examples (such as Doryphoros by Polyclitus) rather than emaciated and withered. It was a new interpretation, even in the use of colors that made this proud youth's body palpitate with vitality.

In this room we can see the *Portrait of Guidobaldo della Rovere* by Agnolo Bronzino (Florence, b.1503-d.1572) the Medici family's great portrait painter. It was done at Pesaro in 1531-1532 and the Florentine artist was now free of the polished styles of his teacher Pontormo. The subject is shown in a three-quarter view and close up so that we can concentrate our attention on his face and hands notwithstanding the splendid details such as the dog's head and the armor for which, according to Vasari, Bronzino had to delay the painting while he awaited its arrival from Milan.

Of the seventeenth century works in this room we should mention the *Holy Family of the Basket* by Rubens which was documented in the Villa del Poggio Imperiale in Florence in 1654-1655. The canvas, painted around 1615 is one of the most famous renderings of this subject; it is close to the Italian schools, especially the Virgin's face reflects Parmigianino's style. Another major work is *St Margherita of Cortona in Ecstasy* by Giovanni Lanfranco (b.1582, Terenzo Parma-d.1647, Rome) the painter from Parma.

It was painted in 1622 for the chapel of the Venuti in Santa Maria Nuova at Cortona and purchased by Prince Ferdinando de' Medici. The canvas is one of the finest examples of the Baroque language that Lanfranco developed fully in his frescoes for the church of Sant'-Andrea della Valle in Rome (1621-1627).

And finally, we must call attention to a semi-precious stone inlaid table. This kind of work was much in vogue

Portrait of Guidobaldo della Rovere, by *Agnolo Bronzino;*
above right: **San Giovannino,** by *Andrea del Sarto;* left:
Holy Family of the Basket, by *Pieter Paul Rubens*
(Jupiter Room).

in Florence at the end of the sixteenth century. It shows
two very similar "panels" where stalks of wheat,
grapes and vines entwine around an amphora. Decorative elements such as flowers and animals appear on
the translucent chalcedony background which is ren-
dered even more luminous by silver leaf (partly black-
ened gold), while thin gold threads outline the vases
and stalks. The table was made between 1605-1610 to
original designs by two famous painters of the era
Iacopo Ligozzi (b.1547, Verona-d.1627, Florence) and
Bernardino Poccetti (Florence, 1548-1612). The panels
were originally meant for the high altar in the Chapel of
the Princes in San Lorenzo which was built but never
put into the chapel; in fact it was dismantled in 1779
when the two panels were joined in its current frame of
silicified wood.

The Saturn Room; below: a detail of the ceiling frescoes by *Pietro da Cortona.*

The Saturn Room

After Cortona left Florence, having interrupted work on the Apollo room and leaving the entire cycle unfinished, the Saturn Room was entrusted to his pupil, Ciro Ferri (Rome, 1634-1689). Although Ferri belonged to the master's cultural tradition, he was incapable of executing compositions that were both solid and airy in light and "rarefied" colors. The ceiling frescoes celebrate the apotheosis of the no longer young prince who is led before Saturn by Prudence and Mars and is crowned by Glory and Eternity. Hercules, personifying the prince rises to immortality.

This room contains some of Raphael's greatest masterpieces. The oldest of these is the *Madonna of the Grand Duke.* It got this name from the fact that Ferdinand III, Grand Duke had the painting purchased in Florence in 1799 during his exile in Vienna and kept it with him at all times and "on all his journeys". It is a famous work which was only made "available" to a vaster public after it was placed in the Pitti Palace following the Italian unification (the jealousy with which the Lorraines guarded this painting resulted in its only being seen in prints and engravings). Radiographic examinations have revealed that beneath its dark background, *The Madonna of the Grand Duke* actually shows an interior view that opens to the outside through a window on the

Portraits of Agnolo and Maddalena Doni, by *Raphael* (Saturn Room).

right. The domestic atmosphere of the painting has led scholars to believe that it was done for a private, and up to now unknown, customer. It is dated around 1506, that is when the artist had absorbed much of Leonardo's art as we see from the composition and the incomparable sweetness in the embrace between mother and child whichare enhanced by the dark background.

The *Portraits of Agnolo and Maddalena Doni*, which the Grand Duke Leopoldo II bought in 1826 on the advice of the French painter, François Xavier Fabre can be dated around 1506-1507. The paintings, were commissioned by Doni a wealthy merchant, important figure in the Florentine republic, and keen patron of the arts and artists, including Michelangelo and Fra' Bartolomeo. They reveal a thorough knowledge of Da Vinci's style of portraiture in the setting which highlights the figures while at the same time placing them in an analytically studied landscape that evokes memories of Piero della Francesca. Similar attention is also dedicated to details such as the hair which is reminiscent of Raphael's teacher, Perugino (Pietro Vannucci, b.1445/50, Città della Pieve-d.1523, Fontignano) represented here by his masterpiece *Lamentation Over the Dead Christ*. Painted in 1495 for the church of the Santa Chiara convent in Florence, it was catalogued in the

Villa del Poggio Imperiale as of 1654. The panel is one of the artist's most famous pieces and it laid the groundwork in both the arrangement and the clearly sentimental and devoted accent for subsequent paintings on the same theme specifically the *Baglioni Deposition* by Raphael (Borghese Gallery, Rome) and Fra' Bartolomeo's *Pietà* which is in the Jupiter Room.

Another famous painting by the master from Urbino is the one which was brought to the Pitti Palace thanks to Cardinal Leopoldo de'Medici (1663-1665), the *Portrait of Tommaso Inghirami*, the famous orator and poet from Volterra who grew up in Lorenzo The Magnificent's court. He was also known as *Fedra* in honor of a play he wrote that enjoyed much success in Rome where he lived from 1483 on. An eminent member of the Vatican court, in 1510 Inghirami was appointed prefect of the Vatican library and the portrait probably dates from that year as well. He is wearing a red gown, halfway between the cloak worn by notaries and the tunic used by the middle class and the "clerical" cap worn by laymen as well, the overall image represents the evolution in Raphael's portraits. Compared with the static look that distinguishes the Doni portraits here we have a body in motion: the grandiose pose renders the subject similar to an evangelistic saint and is a useful

The Madonna of the Chair; preceding page: Madonna of the Grand Duke, two paintings by *Raphael* (Saturn Room).

Portrait of Cardinal Tommaso Inghirami; right: Madonna of the Canopy, both by *Raphael* (Saturn Room).

tool for masking his cross-eyed gaze; there is also a good deal of similarity with Flemish painting as it portrays the subject in an ordinary rather than heroic setting. The objects in the foreground also emphasize this aspect, even though they have been repainted, especially the book and its stand.

The room also contains one of Raphael's most universally acclaimed masterpieces, the *Madonna of the Chair*. This much copied work was the first painting to be requisitioned by Napoleon's commissars in 1799 for transfer to the Louvre. It had been in the Uffizi Tribune in 1598 and then moved to Ferdinand's apartments in the Pitti Palace. In the figure of the Virgin we can see some resemblance to the *"Fornarina"*, the woman Raphael loved. At the beginning of the nineteenth century it was believed that this Madonna and the two children was actually a painting of an unknown woman and her sons. The painting's elegance, starting from the clothes (the delicate silk scarf, the turban-like headcovering so stylish among upperclass fifteenth century women) the type of chair itself (used in the Vatican court) contradict the legend and lead critics to believe that the painting was done for a private customer (even the roundel form, destined for private worship) who was most demanding as far as elegance was concerned, perhaps Pope Leo X himself. This is also suggested by the originality of the pose as well: it reveals Michelangelo's influence in the contraposition of the bodies and the

monumental shapes all governed by a sophisticated balance that render it serene and attractive in its religiosity. For these reasons it has been dated around 1513. The panel depicting The *Vision of Ezekiel* originally belonged to the Bolognese Ercolani family and was purchased by Francesco I de'Medici when Agostino Ercolani was ambassador to Florence (1574- 1579). It was displayed in the Uffizi Tribune and then taken to the Pitti Palace after it had been recovered from the booty requisitioned by Napoleon. More or less neglecting the prophet, who is a tiny figure in the background, the artist's attention focuses on the apparition of the Eternal, surrounded by symbols of the Evangelists, and a sky full of cherubs: a miraculous, awe-inspiring vision, nearly abstracted from the rules of perspective which are imposed only by the tree in the middle of the landscape. It is a grandiose composition that reveals much of the artist's style, practically overflowing the the relatively small panel.

The final painting by Raphael in the Saturn Room is the *Madonna Enthroned*, also known as the *Madonna of the Canopy*, because of the throne on which the Virgin is seated surrounded by Saints Peter, Bernard, Jacob and Augustine. It was commissioned in 1508 for the Dei Chapel in the Church of Santo Spirito (Florence), but was left unfinished because the artist went to Rome. It was in the Pescia parish until 1697 when Ferdinando de' Medici purchased it. It was also assumed that

Niccolò and Agostino Cassana had made some additions to it during that period, however, recent restorations (1987-1990) have confirmed that it is solely the work of Raphael's hand even though he abandoned it in a rather early stage. It is an interesting example of Raphael's painting technique, based on a procedure in which the drawing (still visible) is covered by brush strokes that gradually create the volume of the flesh, fabrics and objects. This composition, defined by structural rules that reveal its fine balance, is a forerunner of Raphael's great Roman season.

Andrea del Sarto's *Disputation over the Holy Trinity* dates from 1518. It is yet another painting done for the destroyed Augustinian monastery of St. Gallo, moved to the church of San Jacopo tra i Fossi and then brought to the Pitti Palace in 1626 where it was placed in the apartment of the Grand Duchess Christina of Lorraine. The main figures in the painting are Saint Lawrence and Saint Francis (probably because of the names of the customers who may have been two of the Peri brothers) and Saint Augustine, an important figure for the church and the monastery, and also the author of *De Trinitate*, a basic of theological doctrine. As recently shown in a scholarly study, a reference to Augustine's treatise can be seen in the fact that the dove of the Holy Spirit does not appear next to the Father and Son, instead it is replaced by the great philosopher's interpretation of passages from the Old Testament and Apocalypse, and that is the mass of darkening stormy clouds which are also an "image of the Holy Spirit". Obviously, this is hardly a reassuring vision of the Trinity. The fact that it was even part of the painting reveals the difficulties of those years, striven by moral and religions problems, the fear of the Antichirst and visions of the "finis mundi". This anxiety subtly pervades Andrea's painting: the colors and dramatic debate with St. Augustine as protagonist are a prelude to the development of the Mannerist style.

Disputation over the Holy Trinity, by *Andrea del Sarto* (Saturn Room).

Neoclassical decoration

The seventeenth century fresco cycle by Cortona and his disciple, Ciro Ferri ends in the Saturn Room. Then starting in the Iliad Room begins the series of rooms which, with the exception of the Sala della Stufa, the Poccetti Gallery and the first room in the Volterrano apartment, were decorated after the Grand Duke Ferdinand III returned from exile (1814). These were supposed to have been the the imperial apartments that were never built (except for Napoleon's bathroom) and which Elisa Baciocchi, the emperor's sister who lived in Florence from 1808, had hired the architect Giuseppe Cacialli to execute. A fresco cycle glorifying the French regime had also been planned for the rooms. When the Lorraines returned the plans were obviously modified to celebrate the ruling family in an ideal pursuit of the former Medici tradition. The same artists who had been engaged to work for Elisa Baciocch were hired: Collignon, Martellini, Fedi, Catani and Podestà who were then joined by Luigi Sabatelli, Ademollo, Marini and Bezzuoli. The subject was the munificent patronage of the Lorraine dynasty (Prometheus Room, the Fine Arts Room, the Aurora Room) their return from exile and the apologia of the restoration's policies (Ulysses Room, the Room of Justice and The Music Room). The decorations, which were begun in 1809 by Collignon in the Prometheus Room and completed by Benvenuti in 1828 with the Hercules Room offer many interesting points for reflection on the development of Florentine painting during the first thirty years of the century when two basic artistic trends could be seen. Alongside of neoclassical culture proper which we can see in the variations by Collignon and Catani (Prometheus Room and the Education of Jupiter Room, airy and full of light, and Martellini's The Aurora Room, a more austere and official interpretation) we can also see the introduction of new artistic elements linked to the current of neo-Renaissance purism. The influence of the purist school is visible in the more flowingly narrative tones of Martellini's work (The Ulysses Room). In a figurative and coloristic taste inspired by the classic ideal of Carraccesque painting it enlivens the rigid arrangement – in strict celebrative neoclassical terms – of Luigi Sabatelli's Iliad Room and the Hercules Room by Pietro Benvenuti. And finally, the fact that Jean-Auguste Dominique Ingres (b.1780, Montauban-d.1867 Paris) was in Florence between 1820-1824 was a determining factor in Marini's (Flora Room) and Landi's (Putti Room) convinced adhesion to the neo-Renaissance purist movement.

The Iliad Room and *Lorenzo Bartolini's* statue of Charity; below: detail of the ceiling showing Mount Olympus by *Luigi Sabatelli* (Iliad Room).

The Iliad Room

This room was once called "Sala dei Novissimi" and connected with a chapel that has since been destroyed. It was frescoed by the Florentine painter Giuseppe Nasini in the late seventeenth century and was then remodelled with other parts of the palace at the end of the XVIII century. The frescoes which can be seen today were done by Luigi Sabatelli from 1819-1825. The ceiling has a view of *Mount Olympus with a Meeting of the Gods*, and it is the lunettes with scenes from the Iliad that give the room its name. In the middle there is a marble statue of *Charity* by Lorenzo Bartolini (b.1777, Prato-d.1850, Florence) that he carved for a niche in the Medici villa at Poggio Imperiale. Commissioned in 1817 and completed in 1835 *Charity* was considered too beautiful for a private residence and therefore was placed, first on the ground floor of the Pitti Palace and then in the Palatine Gallery. Its place of honor in the middle of the room is a bit unusual since it was meant to stand in a niche, and this is reflected in the execution.

64

Charity by *Lorenzo Bartolini* (Iliad Room).

and Michelangelo in Florence and the impact is evident mainly in the arrangement of the composition (the three quarter view of the figure) and the volumetric play created by his great mastery of color. The reds and yellows enhance and define the volumes, thanks also to the black edges, the "houppelande" and the Flemish style dark background that combine to offer a formal synthesis of the image in which the smooth skin and the fine, elegant details such as her jewels and the golden hairnet are all highlighted. Not too distant as regards the pose and the creation of volume through the use of color, yet defintely more modest is Rodolfo del Ghirlandaio's (Rodolfo Bigordi, b.1483, Florence-d.1561) *Portrait of a Woman*. Son of Domenico del Ghirlandaio, Rodolfo embraced Fra' Bartolomeo's style at the beginning of the sixteenth century to later become conversational and "domestic" in his painting. By the neoclassical period the close bond between this painting and Raphael's portrait had been recognized to the extent that it was placed alongside of it. Ghirlandaio reflects the monumental trend that characterized Florentine painting early in the XVI century, while maintaining the link with his father's style as regards the flesh tones and definition of details.

Portrait of a Woman or "La Gravida" by *Raphael* (Iliad Room).

The statue also reflects the artist's education: he had studied in Paris with David. Along with Ingres he shared a love for fifteenth century Italian art and was also influenced – especially in this statue – by Canova's works.

One of the most famous paintings in this room is Raphael's *Portrait of a Woman* or *"La Gravida"*. The name derives from the woman's hand resting on her abdomen, almost symbolic of pregnancy; she is dressed in the fifteenth century manner and the religious medal on her chain is hidden by the neckline. In the seventeenth century it belonged to Cardinal Carlo de' Medici and later was added to Cosimo III's collection. The painting was recognized as a work of Raphael only in the nineteenth century; it can be dated somewhere between 1504 and 1508, the years he spent in Florence and it probably depicts a local noblewoman. The influence of Leonardo da Vinci's painting, was fundamental for Raphael in this period. He met both Da Vinci

Left: Assumption of the Virgin; above: the Passerini Altarpiece, two paintings by *Andrea del Sarto* (Iliad Room).

The two large altarpieces by Andrea del Sarto, depicting the *Assumption of the Virgin* were put in this room when the Lorraines had it rebuilt (1828). They now face each other, and both date from the 1520's. The older of the two is the *Panciatichi Altarpiece*, named for Barthlomeo Panciatichi who ordered it for his chapel in Notre-Dame du Confort in Lyon where he lived. The altarpiece never reached Lyon and entered the Medici collections after many vicissitudes; from 1602 it was in the chapel at the Villa del Poggio Imperiale and by 1687 it was inventoried as part of Ferdinando's collection in the Pitti palace. It was never completed because of problems that developed in the wooden support and perhaps also because of the plague epidemic which struck Florence in 1523. The panel, painted between 1522-1525 is the first rendering of the subject from which Andrea del Sarto derived the other *Assumption* (the *Passerini Altarpiece*) commissioned by Margherita Passerini in 1526. Del Sarto worked on it between

1526-1528 (and probably used his wife as the model for the Virgin); and the painting was purchased by the Grand Duke Ferdinando II in 1639. The passage from one version to the other, with but few variations (taken at first glance) if we exclude the figures of St. Nicholas of Bari and St. Margherita of Cortona that were added, shows that the artist reviewed the works of Fra' Bartolomeo: there is an obvious attempt at veiling all naturalistic references (note the less abrupt rhythms in clothes draping the entire figures, the background and mainly the group of angels surrounding the Virgin who is truly an object of veneration) to give the painting a sharper religious accent. The *Passerini Altarpiece* thus became a basic reference not only for subsequent developments in Florentine religious paintings (especially within the context of Santi di Tito's counter reformation culture), but also for the great Baroque scenes in the works of Cigoli and seventeenth century classicism. A canvas dating from about ten years later that we would like to mention is *The Battle at Montemurlo* by Giovan Battista Franco (b.1510 circa, Venice-d.1561). At a young age this Venetian painter went to Rome to study Michelangelo and then to Florence where he met Vasari and Cosimo de' Medici (soon to become Cosimo I). It was Cosimo who commissioned the painting to celebrate his famous victory of 2 August 1537 over the Florentines led by Filippo Strozzi and Baccio Valori. The work strictly adheres to Michelangelo's tenets and is inspired by a complex iconographic scheme aimed at exalting the moral virtues of Cosimo who is raised above all mortals like the new Ganymede, borne to heaven by Zeus' eagle. *The Baptism of Christ* by Veronese is a later and much more famous Venetian painting and it may be the one mentioned in the Pitti inventories of 1688. Thanks to a drawing the painting can be dated around 1575 when Veronese did the large canvases for the Doge's Palace in Venice. The frank, rich and glowing colors reinforce the complex scene in which the artist reproposes an often painted subject.

Christ in Glory with Saints by Annibale Carracci (b.1560, Bologna-d.1609, Rome) dates from the late sixteenth century (documented by St. Peter's Basilica in the background). It was painted for Cardinal Odoardo Farnese who is portrayed as one of the figures in the foreground. The painting coincides with the period in which Annibale and his brother Agostino worked on the frescoes in the Farnese Palace for the cardinal. Together they developed a language which, drawing on the great traditions of Raphael and Michelangelo, created a new ideal of beauty: cultured, ancient and of the Renaissance all at the same time. It is reflected in this painting too where the figures are in classic poses in a spatial context of enlightened clarity and an arrangement that would become a basis for Baroque painting, as we can see from another work in this room, *The Virgin Appears to St Filippo Neri* by Carlo Maratto (b.1625, Camerano, Ancona-d.1713, Rome). This painting, which also belonged to Ferdinando's collection is from the artist's mature period (c.1675). Annibale Carracci's work had a great impact on him and it can still be seen in the classicism that dominates the Baroque scene and governs the equilibrium. *Judith*, the most famous painting by Artemisia Gentileschi (b.1593, Rome-d.1652, Naples) dates from the second decade of the XVII century. She was certainly the most unusual of the few woman painters in the history of art. The painting, done in Florence for the Grand Duke Cosimo II is another rendering of a theme that was a favorite of Caravaggio's and very frequent in Artemisia's circles. Here it comes through at the highest levels of quality, in the ashy skin of man's head, the warm and almost milky bosom of Judith, the serving girl's clothes, and the embroideries on the clothes of the heroine who is still holding the sword.

Another painting from Prince Ferdinando's collection is the *Portrait of a Lady* by Anton van Dyck. It was done in oil on a sheet of paper (from an book of old stories) then put on canvas and enlarged, probably when it came to the Florentine collection. Also known as the *Portrait of the Golden Lady*, because of the subject's sparkling dress, the study is related to the *Portrait of Caterina Durazzo Adorno and Her Children* (now in the Galleria Durazzo Pallavicini, Genova) and it dates from

The Baptism of Christ by *Paolo Veronese*; below: Judith by *Artemisia Gentileschi* (Iliad Room).

Sala della Stufa, detail.

the artist's Italian period, spent mostly in Genova (1621-1627). In addition to highlighting his great technical skill it reveals the understanding of human nature that made Van Dyck one of the greatest portrait painters of his era.

Sala della Stufa

This small room probably got its name from the fact that the terracotta pipes for heating the grand duke's bedroom next door once ran through it, though another version says that it originally was a very warm and sunny "loggia".

The room is entirely frescoed: on the ceiling we can see *Fame and the Cardinal Virtues*, in the lunettes the most famous princes of ancient and modern times painted by Matteo Rosselli (Florence, b.1578-d.1650), one of the first Baroque painters in Florence. The wall paintings, done by Pietro da Cortona during his first Florentine sojourn (1637-1640) depict *The Ages of Man*. It was the success of these paintings that gained Pietro the grand duke's favor and the commission to do the other rooms.

The frescoes begin on the left wall, starting from the door showing the *Age of Gold* and the *Age of Silver*, and then the *Ages of Copper* and *Iron*, to the left and right of the window, respectively. The cycle was inspired by classical literary traditions and shows the continuing degradation of human life and society which, from its original perfect harmony with nature without even the need to work for food (*Age of Gold*) gradually deteriorated. Next came the *Age of Silver* and labor; wars, looting and capturing enemies followed in the *Age of Copper* and it culminated in total barbarity, with violence overwhelming everything, the weak, education and respect for the divinity (*Age of Iron*). The oak in the *Age of Gold*, as well as the small bunches of branches supported by the putti and the garland held by one of the young women in the background had also led to an alternative and opposite interpretation of these frescoes. That its, that they should be read in the reverse order. This would celebrate the magnificent moment in contemporary Florentine history, with the city practically reborn under the reign of Ferdinando II and his wife Vittoria della Rovere. It is also significant that the name Rovere is synonymous with oak and the tree was part of her family coat of arms.

The Age of Gold; below: the Age of Copper, two paintings by *Piero da Cortona* (Sala della Stufa).

The Age of Silver; below: the Age of Iron, by *Pietro da Cortona* (Sala della Stufa).

Sleeping Cupid by *Caravaggio;* below: Judith Bearing the Head of Holofernes by *Cristofano Allori*
(Education of Jupiter Room).

The Education of Jupiter Room

This room too gets its name from the ceiling frescoes by
Luigi Catani (b.1792, Prato-d.1840, Florence). On the
walls he painted the four elements as personified by
Neptune and Amphitrite, Juno, Vulcan and the Earth.

Of the sixteenth century paintings we should mention at
least the panel of the *Entombment of Christ* by Francesco Salviati (b.1510, Florence-d.1653, Rome), one of the
era's great decorative painters. The panel, which was
the model for a painting made for the church of Corpus
Domini in Venice (1539-1540) reveals the influence of
Raphael's Roman entourage as well as that of Giorgio
Vasari with whom he worked on the decorations in
Palazzo Vecchio.

The most important painting in the room is the *Sleeping
Cupid* by Michelangelo Merisi known as Caravaggio the
famous artist who worked during the years bridging the
sixteenth and seventeenth centuries in Rome, Naples
and Malta. It was here that he painted the canvas in
1608 for the Florentine patron, Francesco dell'Antella.
It was purchased in 1667 by Cardinal Leopoldo de'
Medici (who also ordered the existing frame with its
symbols of Cupid such as the bow and arrows); it is one
of the finest examples of Merisi's mature period. He had
already gone beyond the mere beauty of his early works
and through the skilled use of light created a realistic
image of the naked child lost in sleep. It is a highly

unusual interpretation of the subject who can, in fact, only be recognized by the scattered arrows in the foreground and majestically spread wings.

Seventeenth century Florentine painting is represented at its highest levels by *Judith Bearing the Head of Holofernes* by Cristofano Allori and the *Martyrdom of St Andrew* by Carlo Dolci (Florence, b.1616-1686). *The Judith* is probably Allori's most famous painting; the fact that it was in the "Musée Napoleon" also enhanced its reputation. Although unfinished it is the most elegant version of the theme which was very popular among his contemporaries and celebrated in poems by Rinuccini and Marino. The canvas came into the collection at the end of the artist's life. Holofernes' head is actually a self-portrait and the merciless beauty of Judith is a portrayal of Mazzafirra Allori's model and mistress. There are also other versions of the *Martyrdom of St Andrew* which is signed by Dolci and dated 1646 that came to the Pitti Palace in 1818. The Baroque feeling is evident in the theatrical nature of the scene which focuses on the erection of the cross while the saint on the right, in a dramatic dialogue with the Eternal, awaits his death.

Napoleon's Bathroom.

The "Madonna dell'Impannata" by *Raphael* (Ulysses Room).

Napoleon's Bathroom

This small room is the only part of the emperor's apartments in the Pitti Palace that was actually completed. It is a pure example of contemporary neoclassical tastes as reflected in the stuccoes by Pampaloni and the marble sculptures of the Nereids.

The Ulysses Room

The ceiling was painted by Gaspare Martellini (Florence, b.1785-d.1857) in 1815 and shows a scene of *Ulysses returning home.*

The oldest painting in this room is Filippino Lippi's *Death of Lucretia*. She was the Roman heroine who, after being abused by Sextus Tarquinius, son of Lucius Taruqinius Superbus, died and through this rare example of virtue incited the Romans to rebel against the tyrants. The panel forms a pair with another depicting *The Death of Virginia* (The Louvre, Paris). Both were

The Death of Lucretia by *Filippino Lippi;* below: Ecce Homo by *Lodovico Cardi known as "Cigoli"* (Ulysses Room).

originally front panels for wedding chests used by young women to store their trousseaus. They were very stylish in the XV century and were usually decorated with scenes from the classic tradition (such as this one), the Bible or Boccaccio's *Decameron,* but all aimed at celebrating examples of feminine virtue and modesty. This panel, dated around 1470, when the painter worked with Sandro Botticelli, a student of Filippino's father, Filippo Lippi, can readily be traced to a Botticelli drawing. The two Botticelli panels in Boston and Bergamo are, in fact, different elaborations of the two subjects. Filippino Lippi used the brilliant colors and Botticellian elegance with subtle calculation to develop the story. Moving from left to right, there are groups of characters in three distinct episodes against an architecturally symmetrical background; yet our attention is drawn to the center of the picture where the soft landscape behind the three Renaissance-style arches provides the setting for the death scene in the foreground.

The *"Madonna dell'Impannata"* is by Raphael; it derived its name from the "impannata" the paper or cloth-paned window in the background. The painting which was formerly in Palazzo Vecchio in the apartment of Leo X was later moved to the Uffizi and then to the Pitti Palace in 1697 and perhaps hung in Prince Ferdinando's bedroom. It was commissioned by Bindo Altoviti a banker linked to the Roman curia and a brilliant patron of the arts whose property was confiscated after the battle of Marciano, since he had participated in the anti-Medici coalition. The painting had long been acknowledged as being from Raphael's school, but recent restorations (1983-1984) have practically verified that it was indeed done by the master. Judging from the many copies that had been made over the years, after *the Madonna of the Chair,* this painting is the most famous example of Raphael's work in the Palatine Gallery.

The *Madonna and Child with Six Saints* by Andrea del Sarto was painted around 1525-27 for Becuccio Bicchieraio da Gambassi (according to Vasari, Del Sarto had painted portraits of him and his wife in two tondos that have since been lost) an artisan and friend. The painting was already in the Pitti Palace by 1637. The composition, which is clearly based on the *Disputation Over the Holy Trinity* (see The Saturn Room), was done around 1517 and marks the moment in which Del Sarto abandoned the naturalism and Manneristic tensions

Madonna and Child with Six Saints by *Andrea del Sarto;* right: St. John in the Wilderness by *Cristofano Allori* (Ulysses Room).

that delved into the characters' psychology and conceived the religious image in a timeless and immovable context as a true object of veneration.

Three portraits by Giovan Battista Moroni (b.1520 ca, Albina, Bergamo-d.1578, Bergamo) famous for his work done in the Lombard province of Bergamo date from the XVI century. The three paintings, two men and a *Portrait of a Lady* were part of Cardinal Leopoldo de' Medici's collection and the *Portrait of a Lady* had even been displayed in the Uffizi. The painter was highly sensitive to the new demands of the church as imposed by the Counter Reformation (as can be seen from his many altarpieces), and he conveyed the ideals of the sincere art expressed in the religious culture to his portraits. Here too we can see the obvious attempt to reveal the psychology of the figures through a clear optical analysis of the skin tones and clothing. It is similar to Northern painting and quite removed from the contemporary style of Titian's official and celebrative portraits. Moroni's work laid the foundations for subsequent developments in Lombard painting that would also provide the basis for the young Caravaggio.

An interesting note about Caravaggio: the room contains the *"Ecce Homo"* by Lodovico Cardi (Cigoli) who, until the recent discovery of new documents, had been believed to be the winner of a competition held in Rome by Cardinal Massimi in 1606. Caravaggio himself was supposed to have entered the same competition with a painting of the same subject that is now in Palazzo Bianco in Genoa. The new documentary sources have overturned the legend long substantiated by Cigoli's official biographer (his nephew Giovan Battista) and made it possible to establish a new relationship between Cigoli's painting dated 1607 and Caravaggio's *Ecce Homo* done in 1605. The Caravaggio model theory is also borne out by the single drawing relative to the canvas in the Pitti palace in which Merisi's composition is elaborated, and is also evident from the arrangement of the scene. However, Cigoli contrasts Caravaggio's realism with the soft tones and blends of Correggio and the Venetians whom Cardi had studied at length during his youth.

Cristofano Allori, Cigoli's pupil, painted the beautiful *St John in the Wilderness*, which along with the Judith had belonged to Cardinal Carlo de' Medici and was probably painted between 1612-1615. Like the *Judith, St John* is Allori's reaction to Caravaggio's style, in which the modulated balance that places the figure in the landscape leads the artist to an elegant solution between clasical realism and idealism.

The Prometheus Room; below: Portrait of a Young Man Wearing a "Mazzocchio" by *Sandro Botticelli* (Prometheus Room).

The Prometheus Room

The ceiling frescoes by Giuseppe Collignon (b.1778, Castelnuovo Berardenga, Siena-d.1863, Florence) portray Prometheus and the chariot of thc sun.

This room contains several fifteenth century paintings, the oldest of which is the *"Bartolini Tondo"* by Filippo Lippi (b.1406, Florence-d.1469, Spoleto). The roundel portrays the Virgin and Child with the birth of the Virgin in the background and to the right, the lovely scene of the meeting of Saint Anne and Joachim. The painting is an excellent example of Lippi's mastery of perspective especially in these interior scenes which seem to multiply in the geometric puzzle created by the arist. The sense of color and clear light that give shape to both persons and things, the fluid elegance of motion so that the characters seem to be dancing come across as stylistic elements that reflect the frescoes in the Prato Cathedral and make it datable around 1450.

The Portrait of a Young Man Wearing a "Mazzocchio", the fashionable late fifteenth century head covering, is by Botticelli; other names have also been proposed, such as Andrea del Castagno, Piero di Cosimo and Botticini. Authorship of the *Portrait of a Lady*, or *"The Beautiful Simonetta"* (Simonetta Vespucci died very young, she was loved by Lorenzo the Magnificent's brother Giuliano de' Medici, and Pulci sang of her in his "Stanze"), is disputed along with the roundel of the *Madonna and Child with the Young St John* in which the holy picture is pervaded by a subtle restlessness that modifies the spaces and overpowers the figures as in Botticelli's end-of-the-century works.

The *Adoration of the Magi* and the *Martyrdom of the Theban Legion* by Jacopo Carrucci known as Pontormo (b.1494, Pontorme, Florence-d.1557, Florence) date from around 1520 and 1530, respectively. This student

Right: Martyrdom of the Theban Legion, by *Pontormo;* below: the *"Bartolini Tondo"* by *Filippo Lippi* (Prometheus Room).

Adoration of the Child, by *Francesco Botticini;* below, to the left: **The Beautiful Simonetta**, by *Sandro Botticelli* (Prometheus Room).

of Andrea del Sarto fully grasped his master's sense of psychological study of the characters and his use of brilliant colors. In *the Adoration of the Magi* the narrative theme moves along with the figures as they wind their way through a landscape typical of del Sarto, notwithstanding the obvious influence of Michelangelo's painting, especially in the group with the Virgin and Child and Saint Joseph. Still further influences had their impact on the *Martyrdom of the Theban Legion* (or the *Eleven Thousand Martyrs*) painted for the nuns of the Spedale degli Innocenti. In the dramatic and violent portrayal of the martyrdom the painting seems to reflect the Florentine political situation around 1530, the period of the terrible siege that brought the Medici back to Florence and the subsequent purges. Michelangelo's concepts dominate the composition and the individual figures; the context is similar to the descriptions of the cruel martyrdom provided by Northern European tradition that were known to Pontormo who also, was the first great Italian to interpret Durer's prints.

Among the XVII century works we would like to mention *St Francis* by Jusepe de Ribera, known as "Lo Spagnoletto" (b.1591, Jativa-d.1652, Naples), signed and dated 1643 and part of Mattia de' Medici's collection in 1659. The canvas is marked by a strong religious feeling emphasized by the optical hyperrealism that governs the skin tones and clothing which are shown in minute detail down to the white thread on the seams of the habit.

The Corridor of the Columns

This hallway gets its name from the oriental alabaster columns on either side of the door opposite the Prometheus Room. It contains small paintings, mostly landscapes by Flemish and Dutch artists, which had belonged to the collections of Cosimo II and Cosimo III de' Medici. Both grand dukes had a keen interest in northern painting. Famous artists such as Jacques Callot or Cornelis Van Poelenburgh (b.1586 ca.,Utrecht-d.1667) stayed at the former's court. The Corridor has several paintings by Van Poelenburgh dealing with religious subjects in settings with ruins in the background according to the classical style that had developed in Rome in the early seventeenth century.

Right: detail of the Prometheus Room, with the decorated Sèvres porcelain vase in the middle; below: the Corridor of the Columns.

Justice, fresco by *Antonio Fedi*.

Room of Justice

This room gets its name from the ceiling frescoes by Antonio Fedi (b.1771, Florence-d.1843), and it contains mainly sixteenth century Venetian paintings. One of the most important is Titian's *Portrait of Tommaso Mosti* (even though the identity of the subject is a bit doubtful) done between 1520-1525, and inventoried as part of Cardinal Leopoldo de' Medici's collection. This painting has an intense chromatic balance based on dark shades, in the definition of the masculine face and the sumptuous clothing with the silky, soft grey fur that is so natural as to almost be touchable.

The Flora Room

On the ceiling we can see the *Allegory of Flora* painted by Antonio Marini (b.1788, Prato, Florence-d.1861). The most famous paintings in this room are the *Stories from the Life of Joseph* by Andrea del Sarto. The two panels, executed around 1515 were part of the decorations for the bedroom of Pierfrancesco Borgherini and Margherita Acciaioli, along with other works by Bachiacca, Granacci and Pontormo. The series was broken up at the end of the century and the Grand Duke Francesco I bought the two Del Sarto panels for the Uffizi Tribune. The paintings tell the story of Joseph who, after many tribulations caused by the envy of his brothers, is imprisoned and then released by the Pharaoh as a reward for having interpreted his dreams. Andrea del Sarto develops a smooth story notwithstanding some unsettling Manneristic accents that his two pupils Pontormo and Rosso would later draw to the extreme.

Right: **Portrait of Tommaso Mosti,** by *Titian* (Room of Justice); below: **Stories from the Life of Joseph,** by *Andrea del Sarto* (Flora Room).

Stories from the Life of Joseph, by *Andrea del Sarto*
(Flora Room); left: The Three Graces by *Pieter Paul
Rubens* (Putti Room).

The Putti Room

The ceiling was decorated by the neo-classical painter
Landi.

The room contains several Flemish paintings, including
some beautiful still-lifes such as the *Game and Hunting
Tools* by Willem Van Aelst (b.1626, Delft-d.1683 ca),
who worked at the Medici court and specialized in this
type of painting, and the incredibly illusionistic and
spectacular works by Rachel Ruysch (b.1664, Am-
sterdam-d.1750). In any event, the most important
painting in the room is the *Three Graces* by Pieter Paul
Rubens. This chiaro-scuro painting which belonged to
Cardinal Leopoldo de'Medici was probably done around
1620-1623. It is a unique work by the artist, and an
expression of his ideal of feminine beauty in these soft
golden figures, linked in an embrace of warm friendship
and love.

Two paintings by *Domenico Fetti:* Laborers in the Vineyard and The Lost Groat (Poccetti Gallery).

The Poccetti Gallery

We enter this Gallery, which is named after the painter who did the ceiling frescoes, from the Prometheus Room. The decorations were commissioned by Cosimo II when the Gallery was still an open loggia (it was only closed off in 1813).

Here we can see some very interesting seventeenth century paintings: *St Margaret of Cortona Overcomes the Devil* and the two smaller ones depicting *Laborers in the Vineyard* and *The Lost Groat* by Domenico Fetti (b.1589 ca, Rome-d.1624, Venice). Trained in Rome at Cigoli's atelier, Fetti was influenced more by Caravaggio than his own master. He studied fifteenth century Venetian painting and the works of Rubens. These artistic elements are evident in the two canvases in this gallery that were painted after 1622 when Fetti moved to Venice. Gaspar Dughet (b.1615, Rome-d.1675)

painted the four landscapes comprising a series purchased by Leopold II of Lorraine. The landscapes show mythological scenes that provided an opportunity for the painter to create "ideal" images of nature through the use of light colors and balanced symmetries. This brought him fame and recognition among his contemporaries that lasted into the following centuries. Francesco Furini (b.1604, Florence-d.1649) painted *Hylas and the Nymphs*. This large canvas, which was purchased by the government in 1910, tells of the Naiads' (water nymphs) mad passion for Hylas, a favorite of Hercules, who lost his way in the woods. Furini presented the nymphs' feelings in dramatic terms moderated by a soft sensuality that becomes tranquil and yielding in the group on the right.

Hylas and the Nymphs by *Francesco Furini* (Poccetti Gallery).

The Volterrano Apartment

These rooms on the piano nobile were the private residence of Vittoria, Grand Duchess della Rovere.

The first room, the Room of the Allegories gets its name from the ceiling decorations, *The Celebration of Vittoria della Rovere*, by Baldassare Franceschini called Volterrano (b.1611, Volterra-d.1690, Florence) whose name was given to this wing of the Palace even though the other rooms were decorated in the neoclassical era.

This section of the Palatine Gallery houses mostly seventeenth century Florentine art: a school which was long overshadowed by the opulent Roman Baroque style. Recent studies, however, have revealed that it is indeed worthy of interest. In addition to Cristofano Allori's *Mary Magdalene in the Wilderness* we can see works by painters such as Volterrano and his teacher, Giovanni da San Giovanni (Giovanni Mannozzi, b.1592 San Giovanni Valdarno-d.1636, Florence) famous for his frescoes on the groundfloor of the Palace. The link between the two artists is evident in the small frescoes

on tiles *Painting* by Giovanni da San Giovanni and *Sleeping Cupid and Venal Love* by Volterrano done with quick, skillful technique that has been defined as "scherzo alessandrino", to emphasize the grace and even the humor of the characters as in *Venal Love. The Wedding Night*, done by Giovanni da San Giovanni around 1620 (that is, before his Roman journey) for Don Lorenzo de' Medici, brother of Cosimo II, is based on an amusing anecdote; the painting arrived in the Pitti Palace collection in 1637.

The small painting on copper of *Jesus Christ in the Desert* dates from the artist's years in Rome (1623-1624); the landscape surrounding the figures is unusually poetic and very close to the landscape style launched in Rome by Adam Elsheimer, the German painter who worked there early in the century. Another famous painting by Volterrano is the lighthearted *One of Parson Arlotto's Tricks*. It was commissioned by Francesco Parrocchiani and added to Cardinal Giovan Carlo

The Wedding Night, by *Giovanni da San Giovanni;* below: One of Parson Arlotto's Tricks by *Volterrano* (Room of the Allegories).

de' Medici's collection in the early 'seventies. The protagonist of the painting done around 1640 is Parson Arlotto a man who actually lived in the fifteenth century. He had a reputation for being wise, a man of the people, and fond of amusing tricks and jokes. The scene set in the Villa of Mula a Quinto just outside Florence is a fine perspective view of a happy group of diners. The clever depiction, in bright colors was achieved thanks to the use of tempera technique so that it fits perfectly into the burlesque trend of contemporary Tuscan literature that was so popular with the Medici family.

The Fine Arts Room

In this room the ceiling frescoes by Domenico Podestà show Jupiter sending Iris and Minerva to introduce the Arts to man. The primary painter of the Florentine Baroque school, Cigoli (born Lodovico Cardi) is represented by several masterpieces such as *The Martyrdom of St Stephen* and the *Deposition*. The first altarpiece, signed and dated 1597 was probably done for the nuns of Montedomini and required much work as suggested by the many preparatory drawings that he made. The canvas, which includes political references in the emphatic description of the saint's martyrdom (Stephen is the patron of the Order of the same name founded by Cosimo I) is exemplary of Cigoli's work. Through his familiarity with Venetian art and the complex scenographic compositions of Veronese he transformed Florentine painting and launched it on the path towards the Baroque. The *Deposition* was commissioned by the Compagnia della Croce of the church of Santo Stefano di Empoli in 1600 and was completed, after much study, in 1608. It entered Ferdinando's collection in the Pitti Palace in 1690, and it is one of the "highest proofs of the artist's positive and sensitive eclecticism". In the calculated complexity of the composition Cigoli meditates on his Roman experiences which, through the years, brought him into contact with the classicism of Carracci and the lights of Caravaggio. The altarpiece, which even his contemporaries considered a masterpiece, aroused the admiration of Rubens who remembered the master's teachings in the *Deposition* he painted for the Antwerp cathedral.

Cristofano Allori painted the *Adoration of the Magi*, probably for the Fontenuova sanctuary. It is an interesting painting because it is still in the primary stage, and like a large sketch it is filled with freshness and immediacy. It is a fine example of the artist's technique which, even in the early stages concentrates much emphasis on the subjects' faces and hands.

The Room of the Ark

The frescoes by Luigi Ademollo (b.1764, Milan-d.1849, Florence) depict David and the procession of the Ark of the Holy Covenant. The adjacent room contains many miniatures from the Italian and Flemish schools.

Detail of the ceiling frescoes by *Domenico Podestà* in the Fine Arts Room; below: **The Deposition**, by *Cigoli* (Fine Arts Room).

The Hercules Room

The frescoes in this room, which was designed by the architect Giuseppe Cacialli, were painted by Pietro Benvenuti (b.1769, Arezzo-d.1844, Florence) in 1828. They show Scenes from the Legend of Hercules, from the episode of Alceste and Admetus, to the battle with the Centaurs, to his marriage to Hebe up to Hercules' choice between love and glory.

The Aurora Room

The ceiling decorations with an Allegory of Aurora were done by Gaspare Martellini.

Right: Blue porcelain and gilded bronze Sèvres Vase; below: Hercules and the Centaur, detail of the fresco by *Pietro Benvenuti* (Hercules Room).

The Berenice Room

Giuseppe Bezzuoli (b.1784, Florence-d.1855) painted the ceiling frescoes in this room, showing Titus Leaving Berenice. The room contains works by the second generation of Florentine Baroque painters. One of these, the large canvas showing *Joseph and Potiphar's Wife* was done by Giovanni Bilivert around 1620, commissioned by Cardinal Carlo de' Medici. It too was popular among contemporaries and was frequently copied. The theme itself was very well liked by Florentines of the period because of the versatile "worldliness" of the biblical subject where the ambiguity is emphasized by a soft sensual and refined technique.

Room of Fame

Luigi Catani (b.1792, Prato-d.1840,Florence) executed the decorations in this room which contains mostly seventeenth century Flemish paintings.

The Psyche Room

Here we can see paintings done by Salvator Rosa during his Florentine sojourn (1640-1648), and most were painted for Cardinal Giovan Carlo de' Medici. The land- and seascapes are constructed with a fine sense of space and often deal with moralistic subjects such as *Philosophers in a Wood*. It was painted for Marchese Gerini around 1645-1648 and acquired by Ferdinand III in 1818. It marks a crucial moment in Rosa's landscape painting. In fact, he converted an "ideal" landscape into a philosophical context through the figures (according to tradition) of the philosophers under the plane tree. Diogenes stands out among them, as he scorns cynical morality by refusing the last symbol of civilized life and drinking out of his hands, like the child at his side.

Joseph and Potiphar's Wife, by *Giovanni Bilivert* (Berenice Room).

Green Room (Royal Apartments).

THE ROYAL APARTMENTS

The section of the Pitti Palace that we call the "Royal Apartments" is a group of rooms which, since the days of the Medici had been used for court life and ceremonies. The first three rooms, after the Room of the Niches, decorated with sumptuous silk damask from the mid-nineteenth century, are known as the *Rooms of the Fabrics* and were used for court receptions. Next come the queen's and the king's suites, the *Room of Bona*, and the *Tapestry Apartments* which, starting from the seventeenth century, were used to receive "foreign princes".

Rooms of the Fabrics

The rooms in this suite, called by the colors that predominate on their walls, were created around 1630 when the Grand Duke Cosimo III ordered work to begin on expanding the palace façade. Starting from 1620 the court architect, Giulio Parigi, Ammannati's successor, enlarged the original Pitti Palace with three windows on each side (the Red and Blue Rooms). Then between 1640 and 1650 his son Alfonso completed the façade by adding the ground level and following rooms, that is the Chapel (then known as the Alcove), and the current Queen's Bedroom which was previously known and used as the billiard room.

These rooms, inhabited by the Medici, Lorraine and Savoy dynasties were refurnished in the typical, eclectic style of the late nineteenth century--the style of the Lorraine grand dukes and Savoy monarchs, as documented in the inventories drawn up by the royal keepers of the wardrobe.

Green Room

The ceiling decorations, with Luca Giordano's painting of *The Allegory of the Peace Between Florence and Fiesole* (1682 ca), date from 1823 when the room was restored under the direction of the architect Giuseppe Cacialli. With the advent of the Savoys, the room became the Antechamber to the Throne Room without any changes having been made to the 1855 furnishings arranged by Antonio Menicucci, Keeper of the Wardrobe. Therefore, we can still see the chairs, sofa, firescreen, valences for draperies, mirrors and chandeliers carved by Paolo Fanfani, Lodovico Sani and Lodovico Bellini. The table was made in the mid-sixteenth century, and the Medici chest in 1677 (for Vittoria della Rovere) by the German craftsman Amman; the two consoles with touchstone tops were carved in 1784 by Lorenzo and Antonio Dolci, and now support candelbra, vases and an Empire clock.

Of the paintings in the room we must mention the portraits of the *Knight of Malta* by Caravaggio; of Maria Louisa de Bourbon daughter of King Charles III of Spain and wife of the Grand Duke Peter Leopold; of Louis XV, and Maria Leszczynska and their children, the Dauphin and Marie Louise and Marie Anne, in which the girls are portrayed as Flora and Diana.

Red Room

Under the Lorraine rule and up to the Unification of Italy this was the "Chamberlain's Room". Between 1813 and 1823 Giuseppe Castagnoli (1754-1832) decorated the ceiling with *The Glory of Jupiter and Four Allegorical Figures*. When the Savoy monarchs came to Florence the room became the Throne Room. The platform was built, and a late eighteenth century armchair was decorated with the Savoy coat of arms and an eagle. The other furniture in the room was made in 1854 by wood carvers Angiolo Barbetti and Antonio Mazzinghi while the two cachepots on either side of the throne come from the Ducal Palace in Parma.

Blue Room

The stucco work and fireplace in this room were made around 1765, on the occasion of Peter Leopold's arrival in Florence.

It was not possible to obtain the original furniture, made by Barbetti in 1854, since it was taken to the Ministry for Internal Affairs in Rome in 1920. Today one can still see the table with the inlaid stone top made at the Opificio Fiorentino in 1826, some Empire chairs, and the monumental chandelier with carved flowers and fruits made by Crosten around 1697. The portraits of the Medici family along the walls are by Justus Sustermans.

The Chapel

Described in 1662 as the "chapel of His Serene Highness, Cardinal Carlo", the room was transformed into an alcove for the Grand Duke Ferdinando between 1683 and 1685; the work was done by G.B. Foggini.

The room was converted to a chapel in 1765 when the Lorraine court paid G.B. Dolci, the woodcarver who made the altar and "boiseries" that circle the room.

Of the furnishings we must mention the 1697 semi-precious stone frame made for Carlo Dolci's *Madonna*, a wedding gift from Cosimo III to his son Gian Gastone; the late eighteenth century stools from the palace in Parma still covered with the original crimson velvet upholstery with gold and silver embroidery; the neoclassical carved and gilded wood console, and the neobaroque frame with the Savoy coat of arms.

Room of the Parrots

This room gets its name from the eagles (mistaken for parrots by the keepers of the wardrobe) that decorate the wall fabric. The room, which separates the rooms of the Fabrics from the king's and queen's bedrooms, is furnished in the Empire style. The semi-precious stone table dates from the XVIII century. The pattern, on Egyptian nefrite depicts porcelain vases, and like the matching table in the First Parlor of the Tapestry Rooms, dating from around 1797, it was made to models by Antonio Cioci.

The paintings on the walls include *The Fair at Impruneta*, portraits of the Palatine Elector and his wife, Anna Maria Luisa, daughter of Cosimo III and a copy of Carlo Dolci's *Poetry* on porcelain made by A. Costantin at the Sèvres factory.

The Queen's Suite

Sitting Room

Since the Lorraine era this had been the grand duchess's sitting room, and it was redecorated for the same purpose early in the XIX century.

The furniture we see today dates from the mid-XIX century, with the exception of the monumental ebony and ivory cabinet made by Adam Suster in 1704 (with panels and small ivory sculptures by Victor Crosten).

Bedroom

Like the others, this room was also redecorated during the early decades of the XIX century. Under the Savoy reign, it became Queen Margherita's bedroom and was therefore partially refurnished using pieces that had been made for the Tuscan grand dukes earlier in the century, such as the sofa suite and inlaid desk made by Giuseppe Cantieri of Lucca in 1841 or the XVIII century rosewood chests with marble tops. The items made specially for the queen of Italy were the wrought iron canopied bed, the upholstered dormeuse, and the chair with the Savoy arms. The pieces from the Parma palace include the brass-inlaid wood medal rack, the chest with porcelain panels from Saxony and the Louis XV chair with Beauvais tapestry upholstery. The prie-dieu in ebony and semi-precious stones was made by court craftsmen in 1687 and is topped by an XVIII century gilded bronze holy water stoup. The paintings include a copy of Correggio's *Virgin of St. Jerome*, *The Flight into Egypt* by Luca Giordano, and the monumental *Deposition* attributed to Lattanzio Gambara.

Madonna and Child by *Carlo Dolci* (The Chapel, Royal Apartments).

The Queen's Bedroom (Royal Apartments).

The Oval Dressing Room

This room which is also known as the "Queen's Boudoir" was designed by the architect Ignazio Pellegrini between 1763 and 1764. The decorations were done by a group of plasterers from Milan under the direction of Francesco Visetti and the perspective painter Domenico Stagi, who had already worked on other rooms in the palace.

The walls are covered with silk fabric embroidered by Rosa Migliorati between 1781 and 1784. The two consoles were made by G.B. Dolci in 1767 to support two stone inlay panels depicting allegories of water and air which disappeared during the French invasion in 1799 never to be found again. Along the walls are chairs made in 1887, the queen's dressing table and an impressive Empire cheval-glass created by Florentine cabinet makers who worked for the court.

The Round Sitting Room

Work on this room was begun in 1766 and the decorations were only completed in 1775 by Giuliano Traballesi who painted the fresco of the Three Graces with putti in the middle of the room, the panels over the doors with Bacchanals and the eight tondos with dancing figures.

We can still see the eight sofas carved by Lorenzo Dolci in 1775 especially for this room and four mid-eighteenth century consoles from Parma. The various "capitonné" armchairs, mid-nineteenth century work tables, and a writing desk with chair with malachite veneer were presented to the Lorraine grand dukes by the Demidoff family and were brought to the room around the beginning of this century when it became Queen Margherita's study.

The King's Suite

The *Room of the Parrots* leads to the three rooms that made up the private suite of King Umberto I of Savoy and of the Lorraine grand dukes prior to the unification of Italy. Secret stairs led directly to the offices of the Secretaries of War and the Interior located on the mezzanines above and below the suite. The neoclassical stucco work on the ceiling dates from the late eighteenth century.

The King's Bedroom

The room is furnished with the restored eighteenth century bed – valences and portières – decorated with the Savoy coat of arms among entwined acanthus leaves. The nighttable with the initials of Umberto I by F. Morini takes its inspiration from the Empire style, with an inlaid semi-precious stone top from 1771 depicting *The Triumph of Europe* made to models by Giuseppe Zocchi. The prie-dieu that had belonged to the Palatine Elector was made in the grand ducal work-

shops in 1706 to designs by G.B. Foggini, like the bronze and semi-precious stone holy water stoup from 1704 that was also made for the second child of Cosimo III.

The Study

The walls in this room are decorated with silk fabric woven in the Imperial factory in 1770. The three carved and gilded wood consoles and two mirrors were made by court artisans in the mid-eighteenth century while the Louis XV desk and small Biedermeier ivory and ebony cabinet come from the Parma collections.

The Red Sitting room

This was the king's private audience room and is furnished partly with XVII century pieces such as the two consoles, and partly nineteenth century reproductions of Baroque items such as the mirrors, the two firewood racks and the table with the Chinese-style lacquered top.

The Throne Room (Royal Apartments).

After we cross a small *antechamber* with a mid-eighteenth century wall hanging, we come to the *Room of Bona* which gets its name from Bernardino Poccetti's frescoes depicting the siege of Bona in Africa. From here we proceed to the Tapestry Apartment. Previously called the "foreigners' rooms", it has ceiling decorations by Cigoli and other masters.

The Tapestry Apartment

The Room of Temperance

The fresco by Domenico Cresti, known as Passignano (1560-1636), in the middle of the ceiling is an allegory of Temperance. The tapestries on the walls with scenes from the life of John the Baptist are based on monochromes by Andrea Del Sarto in the "Chiostro dello Scalzo" and, were done by Pietro Fevère while the lateral bands and those above the doors were made in Florence.

The room is furnished with pieces from the XVIII century such as the consoles, sofa, armchairs and small desk, and others from the XIX century including the inlaid table made by Federico Lancetti in 1860.

The Room of Prudence (or the "Garden Youths")

The fresco, Allegory of Prudence, in the middle of the ceiling is by Passignano. The walls are decorated with Gobelin tapestries of the "garden youths" made towards the end of the seventeenth century to drawings by Le Brun, portraying *Le Printemps, Le Grand Printemps* and *L'Automne*. The most interesting piece of furniture is the Baroque chest inlaid with different color woods, the only example from the Medici period that has come down to us.

Dressing Room

This small room is also known as the "Allori Loggetta" after the Tuscan painter who did the frescoes in the late XVI century. It was turned into a dressing room in 1854 and was furnished with mid-eighteenth century rosewood veneer chests, the Empire cheval-glass and the dressing table with porcelain accessories.

Room of the Niches (Royal Apartments).

The Blue Room; below: the White Room (Royal Apartments).

First Sitting Room (Room of Faith)

The ceiling fresco by C. Allori (1577-1621) is an allegory of Faith. The three Gobelin tapestries on the walls depict *Earth, Water* and *Fire*, from the series of the Elements, another showing a landscape and seaview and the three above the doors were made by the Medici weavers. The room contains two rococò-style consoles: one dates from the XIX century with a semi-precious stone inlay top with a design of vases made in 1797 to drawings by Antonio Cioci, several mid-nineteenth century stools and chairs and a mid-eighteenth century Neapolitan intarsia of tortoise shell, ivory and mother-of-pearl that was later mounted on its nineteenth century base. The Empire display cabinet in the middle of the room contains valuable items from the grand dukes' collections.

Second Sitting Room (Room of Charity)

The ceiling fresco by Cigoli (1559-1613) is an allegory of Charity. There are several tapestries on the walls: three made in Beauvais, from the *Iliad* series, portray *Achilles Reproaching Agamemnon, Hector Reproaching Paris* and *The Sacrifice of Iphigenia*; two from the Medici tapestry works are from the series of the Elements and represent *Neptune* or *Water* and *Vulcan* or *Fire*. The last two, with winged putti, come from the Medici tapestry works and are used as door covers.

Furniture from the XVIII century such as the console, sofas and armchairs along with the mid-nineteenth century center table and firescreen were used to decorate this room in 1854. The Louis XVI clock over the console has a complex organ-type striking mechanism and was made by Meuran of Paris.

Bedroom (Room of Justice)

The ceiling fresco by Cigoli is an allegory of Justice. The bed, comprised of four eighteenth century caryatids was set up for Pope Pius IX in 1854. The mahogany and gilded bronze chest, probably made by Charles Boulle, the two corner stands made by J.P. Latz between 1745 and 1749, the ornate mirrors, the console, the armchairs and XVIII century writing desk, cheval-glass and Empire dressing table were also moved here at that time.

Going back through the two antechambers we come to the *White Room* decorated in stucco work by the Lombard masters, Grato and Giocondo Albertolli sometime before 1776. From here we return to the main staircase, and conclude our tour.

View of Room 22, with the statue of Victor Hugo by *Gaetano Trentanove.*

THE GALLERY OF MODERN ART

The Gallery is housed on the second floor of the Pitti Palace in the rooms that had been the royal family's apartments until 1920. The exhibits are arranged on the basis of a concept which is philologically aware of historical continuity between the rooms and collections. They are contained in rooms that had been rebuilt for the Lorraincs in the late eighteenth century and then, with fascinating logic, continue in the Winter Apartments and the Palazzina della Meridiana where frescoes by Niccola Cianfanelli depicting scenes from the *Promessi Sposi* (1834) and Giuseppe Bezzuoli with *Le imprese di Cesare* (1836) create a harmonic bond between intellect, taste and the paintings on display. The Gallery's layout offers an eminently Tuscan overview of figurative art from the late eighteenth to the mid-nineteenth centuries. The nineteenth century exhibits comprise the collections of the Grand Dukes, of the City of Florence and various private collections donated to the museum or the city over the years. The most significant of these, from the historical standpoint, belonged to Diego Martelli, Florentine gentleman and friend of the Macchiaioli painters. Most of the nineteenth century works were, however, largely selected by a special committee for acquisitions that, within the

thirty years from 1915 to 1945 created a core of paintings that is homogenous in its critical and esthetic trends.

ROOM 1

The tour of the Gallery begins with works from the latter half of the eighteenth century. The first room houses important paintings such as *Hercules at the Crossroads* (1742) and *Hercules as a Child Strangling the Serpents* (1743) painted by Pompeo Batoni for the Gerini family that later sold them to Ferdinand III of Lorraine. Next to these, there is a delightful picture by Macpherson, a typical neoclassical conversation piece depicting a group of intellectual friends in a room decorated with classical objects and Renaissance paintings. Then there is Wilhelm Berczy's *Portrait of the Family of Peter Leopold* that emphasizes the "family group" while maintaining the official nature of the painting. On the walls there are two large paintings by Gaspare Landi: the first a religious subject *The Holy Women at the Sepulchre* (1816) and the second, inspired by history, *Veturia at the Feet of Coriolanus* (c 1819). Above the doors are the *Sacrifice of Calchas* (1790) by Santi Pacini and *Psyche Imploring the Gods* by Andrea Pierini. To

Two paintings by *Pompeo Batoni:* Hercules at the Crossroads and Hercules as a Child Strangling the Serpents (Room 1).

the left of the entrance door is the *Portrait of Luigi Mansi* and some portrait sketches by Stefano Tofanelli, from Lucca, fine examples of the artist's introspective abilities that allowed him to grasp the intimate sensitivity of his subjects. Pietro Tenerani's marble statue of *Psyche* stands in front of the window.

ROOM 2

This is the first of the rooms that were once the apartments of Leopoldo II's sister, the Archduchess Louise, that can be described as welcoming and elegant. Like the following rooms, this one contains works from the first half of the nineteenth century, from the Congress of Vienna to the final years of Lorraine rule in Tuscany. On the right side an elegant arrangement highlights two of the most important paintings: *Ajax, Son of Oileus*, the last work by Giuseppe Sabatelli purchased by Leopoldo II in 1829 shortly after the artist's premature death. It is a fine example of Restoration culture which, based on the facile identification of the imposing male nude and its literary origins (Book IV of the *Odyssey*) contains a moral lesson, and *Samson and the Lion* painted by Francesco Hayez in 1842. Here the pale nudity of the hero and the detailed attention to the casuality of his body that no longer uphold the Romantic ideal of beauty, bear witness to the artist's quick grasp of realistic trends.

Various genres are represented by interiors, portraits and landscapes. Those definitely deserving mention are

the *Death of Zerbino* and *Isabella's Lament* (1852) by Giuseppe Bezzuoli. The room also contains several portraits by this artist including a youthful *Self-Portrait* done in Rome around 1818 of Nazarene inspiration and the impressive *Portrait of Marie Antoinette of Tuscany*, second wife of Leopoldo II. Painted in 1832, it highlights Bezzuoli's skill in the fine tonal contrasts of whites and blacks which hint strongly of sixteenth century Venetian painting, as do the fiery sunset in the background and the dog in the foreground, an explicit reference to Titian. Another noteworthy portrait is Friedrich von Amerling's *Portrait of a Ciociara*. Finally, there are two Romantic interiors: Matilde Malenchini's airy and lively *Conservatory Interior* (1816) and the severe, mournful *Funeral of a Capuchin Monk* by Vincenzo Chialli (1824), both of which were inspired by the French painter Marius Granet.

ROOM 3

This room contains paintings inspired by Dante, a favorite literary source for Romantic art. Actually, the impressive canvas of *Farinata degli Uberti at the Battle of the Serchio River* (1842), by Giuseppe Sabatelli commissioned by Niccolò Puccini and then bought by Leopoldo II is based on Scipione Ammirato's text *Istorie fiorentine*. The painting, which concentrates the drama of the episode in the protagonists' figures, reveals the artist's great familiarity with contemporary French painting, especially the works of Géricault. To the left the *Buonconte da Montefeltro* by Gabriele Smargiassi, purchased by Vittorio Emanuele II at the National Exhibition held in Florence in 1861, evokes the poetry of John Martin in the fantastic landscape. A much earlier painting by Andrea Pierini is *Dante at the Court of Guido Novello*. On the opposite wall, next to two pieces by Carl Vogel von Vogelstein showing *Dante and Ten Episodes from the Divine Comedy* (1842-1844) and Goethe's *Faust* (1854-1855) we must mention *Nello at the Tomb of Pia* by Enrico Pollastrini dated 1851. In its sobriety, the painting's colors, and lucid, clear style fully reveal the protagonists' state of mind.

Right: **Samson and the Lion** by *Francesco Hayez* (Room 2); below: Buonconte da Montefeltro, by *Gabriele Smargiassi* (Room 3).

ROOM 4

The dominant painting in this room is *Eudore and Cimodoce* by Luigi Mussini. Taken from *Martyrs* by René de Chateaubriand it brings to life the noble soul of the young Christian, Eudore, who unhesitatingly helps a slave, causing consternation to the young Cimodoce. Painted in 1855 after a sojourn in Paris, it reflects the artist's adhesion to the *Art pour l'Art* movement and the consequent influence of Ingres' young pupils, especially Hyppolite Flandrin. The room also houses works on religious subjects; some are neoclassical like *Sinite parvulos* by Pietro Benvenuti, but most are typical of the Tuscan purist culture. In addition to the series of sketches by Giacomo Conti, the painter from Messina who lived in Florence until the 'thirties, one of the most enchanting of all is Vogel von Vogelstein's *Sinite parvulos venire ad me*, clearly inspired by Biedermeir. The marble bust of Christ, *Salvator Mundi* (1837) by Pio Fedi was definitely influenced by the Nazarene artists.

ROOM 5

This room, too, contains paintings inspired by historical events or literature such as *The Two Foscari* by Francesco Hayez, based on Byron's tragedy. Painted in 1853 for Andrea Maffei, it one of the four versions of the subject by the artist: it focuses on the dramatic moment in which the young Foscari is condemned to death by his father in a loggia of the Doge's Palace in Venice, in the softly illuminated mist of the Lagoon. Two paintings by Baldassarre Calamai are also inspired by literature: two scenes from the *Decameron: The Plague of Florence* dated 1836 and *Boccaccio Tells a Tale in Villa Schifanoia* (1844) that had once belonged to Leopoldo II. Niccola Cianfanelli's sketch of *Lucia and the Innominato*, for the frescoes of scenes from the *Promessi Sposi* which he painted on the ceiling of the Meridiana in the Pitti Palace in 1834 is also on a literary theme. Then there are paintings of famous men, another favorite nineteenth century theme. We can mention *Torquato Tasso Reads His Poem to Eleanora d'Este* (1840) by Cesare Mussini; *Cimabue and Giotto* (1847) by Gaetano Sabatelli set in a landscape described with "northern" coldness according to the current trends of Italian painting, and finally Giuseppe Fattori's large canvas, *Brunelleschi and the Egg* (1845). Another noteworthy painting that celebrates a famous man and depicts a real historical event is Gaspero Martellini's *Lorenzo the Magnificent Lands in Naples* (c 1840). In the middle of the room is a bronze statue of the *Discovery of America* by Aristodemo Costoli (1848), commissioned by Leopoldo II on a plaster model submitted in the Genovese competition for the monument to Christopher Columbus.

ROOM 6

This intimate little room was once the private boudoir of the Archduchess Louise. The ceiling is decorated with flying putti and the back wall is adorned with a large, gilded and carved mirror. The paintings in this room match its overall mood: they are mainly landscapes and figurative works that typify the mid-nineteenth century Romantic era. Giovanni Signorini's works dominate this room. From the early 'forties he worked for Leopoldo II, painting dramatic scenes of natural events such as the

Eudore and Cimodoce by *Luigi Mussini* (Room 4); below: Torquato Tasso Reads His Poem to Eleonora d'Este, by *Cesare Mussini* (Room 5).

Brunelleschi and the Egg by *Giuseppe Fattori* (Room 4); below, right: Bust of Napoleon, from
Antonio Canova's workshop (Room 7).

two versions of the flood of the Serchio River (1844)
and views of Florence and its feastday celebrations:
Fireworks on the Feast of St. John (1843), *The Chariot
Race in Santa Maria Novella*, *The Race in Prato*,
Berlingaccio in Piazza Santa Croce and the *Night of the
Epiphany* that were all painted between 1844 and 1846.
Signorini is also the author of the *View of Florence from
Monte alle Croci* (1857): a delightful harvest scene is set
against the enchanting sunset that illuminates the city's
towers and domes and the Arno river with pink and
gold reflections. Going back through the first room we
continue our tour.

ROOM 7

Here we find typical examples of Neoclassical art inspired by Napoleon and which give an excellent idea of the international nature of Florentine culture in the eighteenth and nineteenth centuries. The room is dominated by the *Oath of the Saxons* by Pietro Benvenuti, commissioned by Napoleon's chief of staff in 1812 when the artist was Director of the Accademia di Belle Arti in Florence. It shows the Emperor receiving homage from the enemy troops after his victory at Jena. The moonlight filters through the clouds, illuminating the peaked roofs of the city, creating a psychological impact as well as an attractive scene. Another homage to the Emperor is the *Bust of Napoleon* by Canova's assistants; the master himself did the *Calliope* (1812) which dates from the same year as the *Venus Italica* sculpted for Elisa Baciocchi (Florence, Palatine Gallery). This wonderful period in Florentine history is further evidenced by the portraits done by François-Xavier Fabre, especially the one of Antonio Santarelli, the artist who did the wax models in the room. Another noteworthy portrait is the one by Louis Gauffier depicting the French artist with his family (1793) against a classical setting. Then there are several landscapes, one by Nicolas DidierBoguet, in Poussin's style, painted in Rome (1792) and another by Wutki showing the artist with two friends keeping him company as he sketches the Aniene waterfall at Tivoli.

Two sculptures by *Giovanni Dupré:* opposite: **Cain**; below: **The Dying Abel** (Room 10).

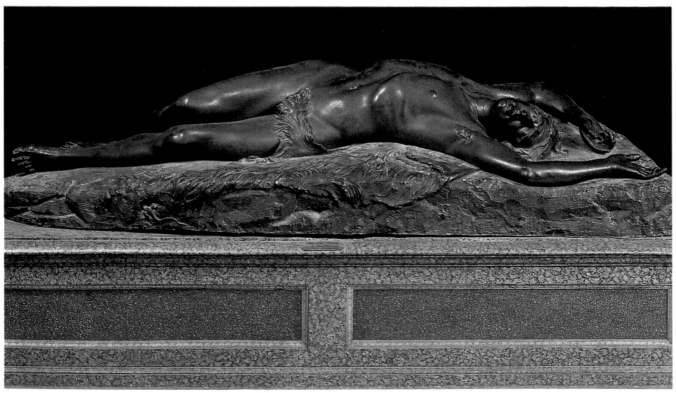

Florentine Story Writers of the 14th Century, by *Vincenzo Cabianca* (Room 11).

ROOM 8

This room contains iconographic works portraying those who ruled in Tuscany between the eighteenth and nineteenth centuries: the Hapsburg-Lorraine, the Bourbons of Lucca, Maria Luisa d'Este, Duchess of Massa and Elisa Baciocchi, Napoleon's sister who is shown during a ceremony in the Loggia dei Lanzi in Piazza Signoria specially decorated for the occasion with blue cloth bearing French lillies. The lapislazuli and pearl dish was also made specially for Elisa Baciocchi by the Opificio Fiorentino delle Pietre Dure.

ROOM 9

In this room we find works directly connected to the Demidoffs, one of the many foreign families that settled in Florence during the nineteenth century. In the middle of the room is the model for the *Monument to Nicola Demidoff*, commissioned by his son Anatoli and executed by Lorenzo Bartolini in 1839; the original stands in Piazza Demidoff in Florence. Nicholas Demidoff was a wealthy Russian who settled in Florence during the Restoration. His philanthropic gestures included the establishment of a home for foundlings and unwed mothers. At the apex of the group stands Nicholas, affectionately surrounded by his beneficiaries; the four corners of the base are the allegories of the virtues, with the most poetic and typical example of romantic thought being *"Charity"*: a mother holding an emaciated little boy, in a pathetic pose reminiscent of The Deposition, with a little girl whose hand on her brother's tiny foot is a distraught and moving gesture. On the walls, two large portraits: on the right Anatoli in exotic costume by the Russian painter Karl Pavlovic Brjullov and on the left, in a fine carved and gilded wooden frame, *Matilde Bonaparte Demidoff* by Ari Scheffer. The lady is portrayed in a plain dress without jewels, but the simplicity of the neo-sixteenth century costume and the pose which echoes Raphael's style impart an air of great nobility to Napoleon's neice. Along the walls there are several marble busts, three are by Hiram Power the American sculptor who lived in Florence and was much admired by the international community. There are two watercolors by Fortuné de Fournier which along with several photographs portray the splendor of the Villa Demidoff at San Donato in Polverosa.

The room is furnished with a writing desk and armchair overlaid with malachite in the Northern European style and a chest decorated with porcelain plaques depicting acrobats and minstrels.

Self-Portrait, by *Giovanni Fattori* (Room 13).

ROOM 10

The main wall is taken up by Giuseppe Bezzuoli's large painting, *Charles VIII Enters Florence*. Commissioned in 1828 by the Grand Duke Ferdinand III of Lorraine, this painting is a majestic example of Romantic art. It is based on a literary subject, Benedetto Varchi's *Istorie fiorentine* and shows a famous episode in the history of the Florentine Republic governed by Pier Soderini: Pier Capponi gets ready to ring the bells in response to provocations by the French King who was summoned to Italy by Pope Alexander VI. The man, in the red tunic, is surrounded by a group of Florentine nobles and intellectuals including Niccolò Macchiavelli and Girolamo Savonarola. The monumental dimensions of the canvas allowed Bezzuoli to narrate the episode by harmoniously alternating historical, moving, amusing, and didactic elements to express the truth behind the event in keeping with Romantic thought, and at the same time show off the elegance of his painting, highlighted by beautiful faces and sumptuous colors.

Opposite the painting are two plaster statues: on the left *Meneceus* (1830) by Aristodemo Costoli, and on the right a *St. Sebastian* by Pio Fedi. The latter, done in Rome in 1843 is exemplary of the demand for particularism that characterized European culture in the eighteen-forties and of which one of the first examples was Giovanni Dupre's *Cain and Abel* (1842), cast in bronze for Leopoldo II in 1851. Another work executed

for Leopoldo II is Enrico Pollastrini's large painting of *The Flooding of the Serchio River* in which the artist shows a farmer rescuing a woman and her child, raising the subject to the level of a historical work. On the left wall is the *Defeat of Frederick Barbarossa at Legnano* by Amos Cassioli, completed in 1870 following the sketch that he submitted for the 1859 Ricasoli Competition. The huge battle scene is dominated by the two protagonists, Alberto di Giussano, with dark hair and firey black eyes and the fallen Barbarossa, impotent in defeat.

There are also some portraits in the room: a *Self-Portrait* and the *Portrait of Aristodemo Costoli* by Giuseppe Bezzuoli, and a *Self-Portrait* by Luigi Mussini.

ROOM 11

Once again the theme is historical subjects, but with emphasis on stylistic research in the Florentine artistic environment. To the left, flanked by small paintings and sketches, is *Medieval or*, the *Exhumation of the Body of Jacopo de' Pazzi* by Odoardo Borrani (1864) in which the artist, in something of a stylistic exercise, handles the historical content with an analytical form that constructs the figures in space according to the rigorous relationship between light and shadow. Further on, is Vicenzo Cabianca's *Florentine Story Writers of the 14th Century*. Displayed at the exhibition of the Società Promotrice Fiorentina in 1860 the painting shows a subject dear to Tuscan culture since the Romantic period, resolved with chiaro-scuro contrasts emphasizing how form prevails over the famous subject to the extent that its importance can almost be defined as abstract. Over the door is yet another painting by Cabianca, *The Breviary* (1862) in which the artist created an impressionistic scene of tranquility playing with the shadow of the church projected on the sun-bleached courtyard facing the sea.

On the next wall are sketches of historical scenes painted with "patches" of color and some portraits by Stefano Ussi, including one of his wife, Linda (c 1858) similar to the chiaro-scuro and lively colors of Cabianca's *Novellieri*.

ROOM 12

The ceiling is decorated with a fresco by Giorgio Berti of *Cincinnatus Receiving the Roman Senate* (1827).

In this room there are several portraits from the second half of the nineteenth century: some of the intellectuals and political figures who contributed to the nationalist cause, commissioned by royalty such as the *Portrait of Francesco Domenico Guerrazzi*, painted by Antonio Ciseri after the writer's death. Others were commissioned by private citizens and at times these are more expressive since the artists were not conditioned by the "official" nature of the representations. Most of the portraits are by Ciseri and his pupils, one of the most noteworthy among these is the *Portrait of Emilio Zocchi* by Raffaello Sorbi, a young man at the time, shown with firey passion; and a great mastery of color impresses himself on the viewer, a very close view of his face with a red hat that leaps out against his pale complexion. Of the portraits by Antonio Ciseri, a Ticinese student of Giuseppe Bezzuoli who became a painter of holy subjects in addition to being a famous portraitist, there is the beautiful portrait of his brother (c 1854), the unfinished, rounded face of a woman called "Ballerina" and that of a *Spanish Physician* (1862). This is an intensely realistic painting in which the man's pale face contrasts with his raven black hair and cravatte in a tonal relationship that deliberately evokes seventeenth century Spanish art. And finally, the portrait of the sculptor Giovanni Dupré, dear friend of Ciseri as the painting itself reveals. Notwithstanding the imposing presentation, Dupré's penetrating, yet smiling gaze seems affectionately directed towards the painter.

Room 12 leads to the Ballroom designed by Pasquale Poccianti in 1801 for the Bourbons, and never completed. Above its four doors there are portraits of the members of the Hapsburg-Lorraine dynasty, the Emperor Franz Joseph and his wife Elizabeth of Bavaria by Giuseppe Sogni; the portraits of the Grand Dukes of Tuscany, Leopoldo II and Marie Antoinette of Lorraine are by Carlo Morelli.

ROOM 13

The ceiling fresco by Nicola Monti shows the *Triumph of the True Cross* (c 1820). This room, too, contains portraits, and perhaps some of the most famous examples of nineteenth century Tuscan painting. The works by Giovanni Fattori are: his intense *Self-Portrait* (1854) in which the artist depicted himself with a proud face illuminated by the stark white of his shirt collar and mussed dark hair which seems to come away from the bluish-grey background; the *Young Man* (perhaps his cousin) painted in Livorno in 1865 that clarifies Fattori's figurative research in the realm of portrait-painting, and the oval picture of *Mrs. Biliotti*, which through its subdued tones and execution transmit the woman's emotional depth. Antonio Puccinelli painted the *Portrait of Mme Morrocchi* around 1858; this dignified and melancholy noblewoman stands out against the silk moirée wall, and her pale face, framed by dark hair, is studied with analytical determination. The fur, a sign of her economic status, takes on a subtle meaning of reassuring comfort that she can hide behind, as the painting's introspective character would suggest.

Alongside are the *Portrait of Giulia Tempestini Kennedy* that Giovanni Boldini painted during his Florentine sojourn and a portrait of *Augusto Betti*, in a familiar, elegantly disenchanted pose, in the style that Amos Cassioli refined in Rome during the 'fifties when he frequented the *pensionnaires* of the French Academy, especially Edgar Degas. On the opposite wall is *Maternity*, a portrait of the wife and daughter of Desboutin, a gifted French painter who lived in Florence for many years and made his villa at Bellosguardo a gathering place for his intellectual compatriots and the Macchiaioli artists he befriended. The room also contains some sculptures by Giovanni Bastianini, including the *Little Boy Fishing* which attests to the artist's international taste: he died young and was best known for his imitations of the Renaissance style.

ROOM 14

The ceiling frescoes showing Virgil's *Tu Marcellus Eris* were painted by Gaspero Martellini around 1829.
The paintings on display illustrate the Tuscan landscape genre in the sixth decade of the nineteenth century from

Portrait of Madame Morrocchi, by *Antonio Puccinelli* (Room 13); below: Portrait of His Stepdaughter, by *Giovanni Fattori* (Room 23).

Confidences, by *Cristiano Banti* (Room 15).

the establishment of the "Scuola di Staggia" in the early 'fifties to the National Exhibition held in Florence in 1861. The Staggia painters included two Hungarian brothers, Carlo and Andrea Markò (two noteworthy works by the latter are the *View of Monte Forato* left of the window, and the *Carbonai*, dated 1861, hanging over the fireplace), Emilio Donnini (the painting of the *Ironworks of the Principe Corsini*, is significant for its "positivist" interest in industrial development), and Serafino De Tivoli, who was also interested in the luministic studies of the Barbizon school. He was even more profoundly affected by them after his tour of the 1855 International Exposition in Paris, as we can see from his *Pasture* (1859), clearly a tribute to Rosa Bonheur and Troyon whose Florentine reputation was also strengthened by Giuseppe Palizzi, the artist from Puglia who lived in Paris. In his painting *In the Heart of the Forest* (1845) the light makes a path between the branches and breaks the forest undergrowth into fragments. This room also contains two large canvases by Antonio Fontanesi: *After the Rain*, 1861, in which with apparently quick and light-filled brushstrokes, the artist recreates the crystalline atmosphere of a mountain landscape, and the twilight melancholy of *Shepherds*, painted about twenty years later.

In the middle of the room stands a marble *Flora* by Giovanni Dupré (1869) that was most probably made for Ferdinand, son of the former Duke Leopoldo II.

ROOM 15

This small room is decorated with paintings by Luigi Catani, dating from around 1825, that commemorate famous scientists and philosophers.

Also on display are paintings from the collection of Cristiano Banti, most of which were donated to the Gallery by one of his heirs. Almost all of them are by Banti and Giovanni Boldini and were painted in the Banti country home, showing members of the family or country scenes.

Some of Boldini's most noteworthy paintings include the portraits of Alaide Banti at various stages in her life: a sweet, somewhat affected little girl in a white dress; a fascinating woman smiling gaily at the artist who had by this time moved to Paris where he developed his "saberstyle" brush strokes that would make him a famous portrait painter of lovely Parisian ladies. Cristiano Banti's paintings include works such as the *Peasant Women at Montemurlo*, a fine example of the figurative studies by Tuscan artists in 1860 when they began painting "spots" of light according to rigorously analytical methods. Then there are fine later works such as the *Woodcutters, Confidences* and *Three Peasant Women* that reflect the artist's interest in a more intimate type of art partly influenced by André Breton's naturalist paintings. Banti met Breton during one of his frequent stays in Paris. Another important painting in the collection is a small portrait by Saverio Altamura (1853), the girl's graceful delicacy and melancholy reflect the artist's interest in the pre-Raphaelite movement.

ROOM 16

Also decorated by Luigi Catani with allegorical paintings of philosophical subjects, this room contains the collection once owned by Diego Martelli, the art critic and supporter of the Macchiaioli painters. The collection contains outstanding works revealing their figurative studies, some of which were painted at Martelli's estate in Castiglioncello such as *Before the Storm* (c 1862) and *Houses at Castiglioncello* (1864) by Giuseppe Abbati and *Laundry in the Sun* by Raffaello Sernesi. *Boys Stealing Figs* was also painted by Sernesi, with great skill he creates a feeling of absolute happiness in the boys stealing fruit on a late and sunny summer morning.

The lovely portrait of Teresa Marelli is by Odoardo Borrani: its subdued style highlights the lyricism of Macchiaioli painting with emphasis on even the simplest everyday expression, critically observed through meticulous analysis. Over the fireplace hangs one of the most famous paintings from Fattori's mature period: *Roman Carts* (c 1872) a fine of example the artist's constant studies where he creates unsettling space by altering the perspective relationship: cutting out part of the white wall, breaking its linearity with the rhythmic lines of the black cloaks of the carters. Fattori's narrative rigor was such that at an advanced point in the painting he eliminated the figures that would have made it too "conversational". Alongside hangs the painting of *Mrs. Gioli at Fauglia* (1875) which Fattori did on his return from Paris where he admired the works of Corot as suggested by the view of the young woman in the blue dress between the vertical lines of the trees. Between the windows we can see some paintings from Fattori's later years when he experimented on rougher and more melancholy themes. In the middle of the room on a table inlaid with semi-precious stones is a terracotta statue *Nana*, done by Adriano Cecioni in Paris during the early 'seventies.

On the far wall, two paintings by Pissarro, *The Storm is Drawing Near* and *Trimming the Hedges*. Martelli bought them in Paris and had them sent to the Florentine Promotional Show of 1878, and *In Bed* by Federico Zandomeneghi, the artist who painted the two

Mary Stuart at Crookstone, by *Giovanni Fattori* (Room 17).

Singing a Stornello, by *Silvestro Lega* (Room 17).

monumentality the artist was able to transmit to an exquisitely domestic subject.

Between the door and window are some works by Giuseppe Abbati including *The Cloister of Santa Croce* (1864) and *The Oration* (1867). The first is practically a "poster" of Macchiaioli art: a small panel in which with a few essential words the artist conveys the stone-cutter's tranquility during the hottest time of day. *The Oration* is a painting awash with melancholy, the formal rigor of the young woman praying at a tomb inside a church has no false grace. The subject is similar to the statue, *A Visit to the Graveyard* by Adriano Cecioni, done in Naples in 1865 while still a student. Cecioni also sculpted the moving *Suicide* in 1867, in Naples. The two smaller statues, *First Steps and Boy with a Rooster*, date from the late 'sixties and both reflect the precarious cultural situation of that change-filled period.

In fact, both show small children in transitory situations; they are modelled along a line that breaks and moves to suggest fragmentation of the equilibrium as well. The intense and melancholy *Portrait of the Artist's Wife* (fireplace wall) also dates from that period when Cecioni, who had returned to Florence, was seeing the painters of the Piagentina school. Other noteworthy paintings on the same wall are *On the Shores of the Ofanto River*, by the young Giuseppe De Nittis, dating from the early 'sixties and *The Hunting Party* by Filippo Palizzi, also done while the artist was young, and narrated with charming skill. The room also has views of the city, with the most important ones being the *Feast of 27 April 1859* by Enrico Fanfani (above the exit door) and a *View of the Old Market* by Giuseppe Morrici dated 1862.

ROOM 18

The ceiling was painted by Antonio Luzzi, about 1825 and shows *Achilles Taken by His Mother Thetys to See the Centaur Chiron*.

In this room we can see paintings illustrating various episodes in the Risorgimento, many commemorating battles fought for the unification of Italy, but also sensitive to human drama such as the departure of the conscripts (I. Affanni *The Conscript*, c. 1862), or the anguish of the soldiers' families (G. Morrici's *Letter from the Soldier in Garibaldi's Army*, 1861). Perhaps the most important painting in the room and the finest example of Tuscan culture in that period is *The Italian Camp After the Battle of Magenta* by Giovanni Fattori (1862). The painting, completed after many drawings and preliminary studies, is Fattori's first work based on contemporary events. It commemoratres the battle fought in June 1859 that determined the Italian victory in the second war of independence.

Fattori, without emphasizing the fighting, focused attention on the back lines where tired, dusty soldiers and officers stand aside to make way for the cart carrying the wounded. The scene is a desolate landscape (the artist went to Magenta in the summer of 1860) where the clear, pale light reaches to the horizon, and the outlines of the city are lost in the mists of the Po Valley. The painting was presented at the First National Exhibition in 1861 even before it was completed.

portraits of Martelli that are above the doors. One door leads to a small room with mementoes of Ugo Foscolo, a very dear friend of Quirina Mocenni Maggiotti, Diego's great-aunt; the other door is the way out.

ROOM 17

The ceiling fresco by Giuseppe Bezzuoli shows *Alexander in the Studio of Apelles*. The artworks in this room illustrate different trends in nineteenth century Italian painting. On the left are some historical paintings; the most important in this group is *Mary Stuart at Crookstone* (1861) by Fattori, executed with "macchiata" technique and marked chiaroscuro contrasts in keeping with the Florentine trend of the period following the examples of Altamura and Morelli in an attempt to refresh the historical genre.

On the righthand wall we can see Domenico Induno's *Usurer* (1853) that was exhibited at the Florentine Promotional Show and *Joys of a Mother* (1866) by Gaetano Chierici, an apparently sweet potrayal which barely masks an uneasy state-of-mind deriving from the rapid changes in modern life, and finally Silvestro Lega's *Visit to the Nurse* dated 1873. Lega also painted *Singing a Stornello* (1867), it is one of his most famous works, if not his masterpiece. It was admired from the day of presentation because of the fifteenth century

Another highly interesting painting is the *Barracks at Modena* by Ferdinando Buonamici (1859) where we catch a moving glimpse of the troops in the large, gloomy room, told in a subdued and severe style. And finally, the *Bersaglieri Return After a Reconnaissance* (1860) by Silvestro Lega. The artist considered this his first "effective" painting, that is, in accordance with a formal genre that also emphasized the landscape, and specifically the Macchiaioli.

We now cross the Ballroom again, where opposite the mirror we can see *Susanna* by Odoardo Fantacchiotti and can continue our tour.

ROOM 19

This room contains late nineteenth century paintings of religious or historical subjects. The most important of these are *Ecce Homo* and *Transporting the Christ* by Antonio Ciseri. The latter is one of four versions the artist painted between 1864 and 1870 and shows the pathetic procession, in eastern dress, descending the hill at twilight.

Ecce Homo was commissioned by the Italian Government in 1872 and was only completed in 1891. The almost lifesized painting, in a "historical" setting illustrates the moment in which Pilate showed Jesus Christ to the crowd. The artist succeeded in creating considerable emotional tension, setting the scene on a dimly lighted balcony, forcing the viewer to participate since the main characters' backs are turned.

One of the historical paintings *Conradin of Swabia* is by Egisto Sarri pupil of Ciseri and another, in a carved and gilded frame is Rodolfo Morgari's *The Dying Raphael* (1880). This monumental canvas shows the dying artist entrusting Fornarina to Cardinal Bibiena, a subject that was typical of late nineteenth century bourgeois tastes for anecdotes.

Also of great interest is the bronze sculpture group by Achille D'Orsi, *Parassites* (1872) showing two vile and lowly creatures who, in Roman times lived from day to day at the mercy and pleasure of the powerful.

ROOM 20

The murals on the walls date from the first half of the seventeenth century. They are an allegorical representation of the twelve months and were done by Ulisse Giochi a pupil of Bernardino Poccetti. The room contains sketches and historical paintings that bear witness to mid-nineteenth century Tuscan artists' desire to renew that theme. In addition to the sketches by Annibale Gatti, there is the *Signing of the Treaty of Bruzzolo* by Giuseppe Bellucci (c 1870). The most important of all is Stefano Ussi's *Expulsion of the Duke of Athens* (1861) which was presented at the National Exhibition. It is an example of how the historical genre could be renewed in a realistic key. The historiographical setting in the Bargello and the protagonists' intensely expressive figures – actually Ussi's friends posed for them – fill the scene with a theatrical aura that emotionally involves the viewer.

Sketches of Oriental subjects, many done by Ussi during his travels to Egypt (1869) and Morocco (1875) are also displayed in this room. This genre, which was very

Visit to the Nurse, by *Silvestro Lega* (Room 17).

The Italian Camp After the Battle of Magenta, by *Giovanni Fattori* (Room 18).

popular in late nineteenth century Europe was finely interpreted by Alberto Pasini, perhaps the most famous Orientalist in Italy. He used Mediterranean light to describe scenes and landscapes such as the *Caravan Near the Red Sea* (1864) with a rigorously analytical method.

ROOM 21

Like the preceding room, this one was decorated by Ulisse Giochi; it is dedicated to the House of Savoy and the battles that achieved Italian Unity. Alongside of portraits of Victor Emanuel II and other members of the royal family and furnishings from the Pitti Palace when it was their residence, there are two huge canvases: the *Final Charge at the Battle of San Martino* by Carlo Ademollo, dated 1863 (on the left) and Emilio Lapi's *Battle of Palestro* (1862). Both are the final versions of subjects which the artists had entered in the 1859 Ricasoli Competition. To the right of the window is the *Cavalry Charge* by Giovanni Fattori, dated 1873 in which the perspective is so close that the viewer can almost feel the animals bursting from the canvas.

ROOM 22

This is the first of the suite of rooms that runs along the palace façade. It was remodeled and decorated according to plans by Pasquale Poccianti between 1815 and 1830 and was meant to be the private apartments of the duchesses. The room contains sculpted and painted portraits from the second half of the nineteenth century, mainly by Tuscan artists, as well as some foreign painters such as Carolus Durand who did the big portrait of the woman hanging near the window. The painting is surrounded by charming works by Charles Chaplin and Filadelfo Simi, in which pastel shades enhance the intimacy of the young women in their boudoirs.

In the middle of the room there is an impressive marble statue of *Victor Hugo* by Gaetano Trentanove. The writer is in a classic late-nineteenth century pose: seated in an armchair and thoughtful; his clothing, like the upholstery, is shown in minute detail to the extent that the marble seems ductile. The female busts in the room are worked in a similar style, the drilled marble creates the airy look of lace. The terracotta and bronze statues, mostly by Augusto Rivalta also portray men in poses that allude to the fleeting moment: some, for example are smoking. Of the many portraits by Michele Gordigiani we must mention the young woman with loose hair and a bright sunny smile. To the right of the door a large portrait of a woman by Vittorio Corcos of Leghorn. Here the sophisticated grace of an elegant woman is presented against the poor coastal scene. Alongside we can see a delightful fin de siècle interior by Aldolfo Belimbau: a young, bored woman ignores her

Ecce Homo, by *Antonio Ciseri* (Room 19).

book and lets her gaze wander among Chinese vases and peacock feathers. Another female portrait, by Ulvi Liegi, reflects the artist's interest in the works of Gauguin and Van Gogh.

On the left wall are portraits by painters who were fashionable in nineteenth century Florence: Tito Conti, Federico Andreotti and Edoardo Gelli.

ROOM 23

In this room are works bought by the City of Florence early in this century specifically for a gallery of modern art. It contains some of the most famous and important Macchiaioli paintings, especially Fattori's *The Palmieri Rotonda* (1866). This small painting shows a group of ladies sitting under a sunshade at the sea. With a careful selection of "words" that can also be noted by the changes in the final version, the artist creates an illusion of a fleeting impressionistic glance which is still powerful enough to convey the cultural position, state of mind and even age of the women. *Portico* (c. 1861) by Vito D'Ancona was conceived according to the Macchiaioli method and nearly reduced the view of the sun-filled threshing floor beyond the dark archway to an abstraction.

A series of paintings by the mature Fattori include *The Tuscan Maremma*, exhibited in Florence in 1880; *Lo Staffato* painted the following year in which the an-

guish of the scene is resolved by the impetuous figure of the frightened horse who seems to be running forever as he breaks the horizon line. On the same wall we can see the *Portrait of His Stepdaughter* (1889), a painting of great expressive strength emphasized by the picturesque relationship between the dark-haired girl's heavy features and the fan with red flowers; the *Tired Horse* is a pastel dated 1903, and still by Fattori *Libeccio Wind* (c. 1883), shown with the preliminary sketch.

The large painting of *Sand-diggers Along the Mugnone* (1873) by Odoardo Borrani is typical of the lyricism of the Piagentina period as it blends with the minute details of this urban scene. The paintings by Telemaco Signorini are *Rooftops at Riomaggiore*, where the slate roofs emphasize the graphism, and the harsh *Penal Bath at Portoferraio* (1894) painted in a rugged style that matches the mood of the convicts lined up against the wall for inspection.

The model and final version of the marble statue *The Mother*, by Adriano Cecioni were presented in Turin in 1880 in the hopes of obtaining a government grant for its completion. The sculpture aroused much criticism which Cecioni answered by explaining that the figure was meant to be an ideal and not limited to its appearance as a common woman.

The room also houses several paintings by early twentieth century Venetian artists such as Ettore Tito, Beppe

Two paintings by *Giovanni Fattori:* **Cavalry Charge** (Room 21); below: **The Palmieri Rotonda** (Room 23).

Lo Staffato, by *Giovani Fattori* (Room 23).

Ciardi and Pietro Fragiacomo which were purchased at the Biennial exhibitions in Venice.

ROOM 24

This room contains many paintings from Leone Ambron's collection that he began donating to the Gallery in 1947. Most of the paintings are Macchiaioli, but there are examples from other Italian, and especially the southern schools. In addition to the panel by Antonio Mancini, painted on both sides (the little girl in pink has an intriguing look on her face), there is an enchanting landscape by Filippo Palizzi. It's a small painting showing a field of ripe wheat from so near a perspective that it fills the eye with gold, dotted with the red poppies.

The most noteworthy Macchiaioli paintings are by Fattori: *Diego Martelli on Horseback* (c 1867), *Portrait of the Artist's Second Wife* (1889) and above all, *Cousin Argia* (1861). The young woman in a fine grey dress with a rosebud at her waist sits erectly in a bare room. The light seems to stop and anlayze each detail while at the same time soaking through this lovely picture.

There are sketches by Silvestro Lega dating from around the mid-sixties to the final years when the painter, whose eyesight had weakened, lived at Gabbro inland from Leghorn. In addition to Telemaco Signorini's monumental *Pasture at Pietramala* there is the *Garden at Careggi* and the street scene at *Leith*. This latter work is a memento of his journey to England in the early 'eighties and focuses on the chromatic strength of the red and blue poster among the misty shades of the industrial city. And finally, a painting by Adriano Cecioni from the late sixties depicting a group of children in grown-up clothing which is as lively and amusing as the scene it portrays. Cecioni also did the marble sculpture of the *Meeting on the Steps* (1884-1886). This statue, which was purchased only a few years ago, is comparable to the *Boy with a Rooster* and *First Steps* (Room 17) dated around 1868-1869.

ROOM 25

The melanchony illusion of a world in which life goes by without any abrupt upheavals is the theme that unites many of the pictures displayed in this room. There is also a fine view of Fiesole dated 1868 by Ferdinando Buonamici: it was done during the period he frequented the Piangentina painters. Along with Lega, Borrani, Signorini and sometimes Cecioni, he would go down to the banks of the Africo still untouched by urban progress, and sketch.

At the Fountain (1879) and *To the Fields* (1881) are both by Egisto Ferroni: country life seems a bulwark against the modern world, even though the life of the *Shepherd Girl* knitting will also be marked by the passing train. In Ruggero Focardi's *Country Life*, the awakening of love seems more genuine in a country setting. The two girls and the thin gaunt farmer are backed by a hill where young leaves create a lively flutter- in the divisionist mode-following the example of the Florentine painter Kienerk.

Foccardi also painted the *Bocce Game* (1894): here the skillful arrangement and clear painting style create a vaguely unsettling atmosphere in an otherwise ordinary scene. Two paintings by Telemaco Signorini dated

Penal Bath at Portoferraio, by *Telemaco Signorini* (Room 23).

1892, *Morning in Settignano* and *End of August at Pietramala* are displayed between two of Giovanni Fattori's masterpieces *Market at San Godenzo* and *The Sheep Jump*, both painted in 1887. Fattori got the first idea for *The Sheep Jump* in 1881 during a stay at the estate of the Principi Corsini alla Marsiliano, in Maremma. It is also likely that in addition to drawings he also used a photograph as a basis for the painting; the photograph is still in the Corsini archives. And finally, the huge *Sick Horse*, (1887) by Ruggero Panerai, a pupil of Giovanni Fattori, is very close to the master's work in both subject and style.

ROOM 26

The paintings in this room also focus mainly on Tuscan naturalism, such as the masterpieces *Spring* (c 1891) by Adolfo Tommasi and *In the Woods* (1892) by Niccolò Cannicci. Like the ones in the preceding room, these paintings allude to the difficulties in cultural and ethical identification that swept over Europe during the second half of the nineteenth century. Both of these large canvases illustrate apparently ordinary scenes and si-

tuations, but they are filled with emotional overtones, Tommasi's painting shows some turkeys pecking in an artichoke field, while Cannicci's portrays a child with his puppy: waiting for time to go by each takes comfort from the other. Cannicci also painted *Thirst in the Fields* in 1877, a charming, light-filled canvas executed with tiny brush strokes.

The far wall is dominated by Eugenio Cecconi's monumental painting *Wild Boar Hunt in the Marsh of Burano* (1884). The dogs are depicted with the affection of a hunter who knows his animals, and with a style that exploits the chalky white canvas to give the animals vitality and motion. Another noteworthy painting by Cecconi is the small canvas to the right of the window: a lamp with a red shade casts a glow on the tablecloth creating orange reflections.

Lake Massaciucolli painted by Ludovico Tommasi in 1896 is filled with violet and orange tones suggestive of love for the sun-drenched Mediterranean landscapes which were to soon involve the artist who was attracted by the vitality of Nomellini and the others who visited Giacomo Puccini's villa at Torre del Lago.

Diego Martelli on Horseback, by *Giovanni Fattori* (Room 24); opposite page: Garden at Careggi, by *Telemaco Signorini* (Room 24).

End of August at Pietramala, by *Telemaco Signorini* (Room 25).

ROOM 27

Along with works by Alberto Pisa and Torello Ancillotti, two artists who painted in France at the end of the nineteenth century and Pio Joris that were donated to the Gallery by Leone Ambron, the room contains works by southern artists.

A landscape with many sentimental overtones, by Achille Vertunni is typical of the desire for "truth" that inspired artists starting from the 1840's. Domenico Morelli painted the *Cemetery at Constantinople*, a fantastic image of the city that evokes its exotic nature. The child in fancy dress by Antonio Mancini is a fine example of the painter's poetic skills in depicting the little boy with such a painfully adult expression. The delightful painting of the student by Michele Cammarano, brings to mind characters from contemporary French literature, such as Frederique, in Flaubert's *L'Education sentimentale*, who doesn't have the courage to tell his mother about his failures at the university. Then there is the *Promenade at Capri* by Marco De Gregorio where a clear light, goes through the figures and the landscape, revealing the affinity between Tus-

can and Neapolitan artists in the '60s. In a famous painting by Filippo Palizzi of *Boys with a Donkey* the subject is merely a pretext for the airy form filled by strong brushstrokes, vibrating with light. There are two paintings with the same title, *Shower of Ashes*. One is by Giuseppe De Nittis (1872) and the other by Gioacchino Toma. The De Nittis version, like many Italian paintings of the period emphasizes the power of nature over man who is reduced to mere splotches of color. Toma's painting (1880) on the other hand describes the state of mind and superstitious fears of the people facing a natural phenomenon.

On the wall above the fireplace there is an echanting view of a threshing floor, sprinkled with the light that filters through the treetops, by Mario De Maria.

ROOM 28

This room provides an overview of Italian Decadentism as well as the work of some foreign artists. An exception is Giacomo Martinetti's fascinating picture of *Dianora de' Castracani* (1873). The sparkling light and lively colors endow the subjects with a new vitality in keeping with contemporary Middle European styles. On the left wall are paintings and pastels by the German artist Franz von Lembach along with works by Otto Vermeheren and Adolf Hildebrandt. These two Germans worked in Florence from the 'seventies on, and spread the German love of the Mediterranean as the cradle of myth and beauty. The *Nymph* by Domenico Trentacoste in the middle of the room was inspired by the works of D'Annunzio in the sleepy pose that enhances her beauty. The philosophy was shared by other artists whose works are on display such as Adolfo De Carolis, Sirio Tofanari and Angiolo Vannetti. On the far wall, on either side of the niche containing plasters and other works by Trentacoste (the Gallery has a vast number of works by this artist that were donated by Ugo Ojetti in 1933), are two large female portraits. On the left a very "à la page" lady in a cozy art déco room by Roberto Pio Gatteschi; and on the right a typically "belle epoque" portrait by Edoardo Gelli in an elaborately gilded wood frame decorated with mermaids swimming among water lillies. Next to a portrait of Galileo Chini by Sirio Tofanari are three panels by the ceramist, inspired by Oriental themes, *Faith, Peace* and *Indolence* which Chini painted during his 1912 sojourn in Siam where he was summoned to decorate the royal palace in Bangkok. Over the exit door we can see *Fireworks in Venice* by Guido Marussig, and to the left of the window an intense *Self-Portrait* and various small paintings by Filadelfo Simi, including *An interior at Alhambra*, where the tiled courtyard creates a feeling of cool shade on a summer afternoon.

ROOM 29

This room contains works illustrating the main artistic trends from the end of the nineteenth and early twentieth centuries. Divisionism is represented in all its versions: melancholy, dreamlike, "social" and vitalistic, by several fine works. Two by Gaetano Previati are *In the Meadow*, (1889-1890) an enchanting image of children next to a rose trellis that rises to the sky, and the large drawing for the *Hostages from Crema* (1878-1879). Other fine works are Vittorio Grubicy's *Ancient Shepherd* wrapped in the pinkish twilight mists (1888) and *Spring Garden* by Carlo Fornara, with its full-bodied brush strokes. Alongside is the *Landscape* by Giorgio Kiernerk, that practically lets us feel the fragrant green leaves of the treetop set against the blue sky. On the opposite wall, along with works by Emilio Notte and Giuseppe Mentessi is Angelo Morbelli's *I Remember*

Promenade at Capri, by *Marco De Gregorio* (Room 27).

Shower of Ashes, by *Giuseppe De Nittis* (Room 27).

When I was a Child (1903): a melancholy theme that expresses the feeling of illusory individual dignity through the solitude of old-age, and which is similar to *The Bowl of Soup*, the large plaster statue by Domenico Trentacoste (1904) in the middle of the room.

Vitalistic expressions are evident in the works of Plinio Nomellini painted during his sojourns in Versilia: *Small Bacchus* (c 1908) actually a portrait of his son Vittorio, with the graceful nudity of his infantile body surrounded by sunlight and the abundance of the grapes. *First Birthday* (1914): a celebration for a little girl whose mother leads her into a large room facing the Apuan Alps where a bicycle leans against the wall. And finally, the lovely *Portrait of Lorenzo Viani*, a fleeting apparition of the painter's sensitive face amongst the trees. Viani's *Self-Portrait* dated 1912 is also displayed here: the face is sweetened by the daisy pinned to his coat. Four sculptures by Medardo Rosso reveal the artist's poetic skills; the subjects range from the melancholy and very human *Child at the Kitchen Stove* (1892) and the *Doorwoman*, a delicate wax model from 1883, to the vitalistic *Woman Laughing* (1891) whose face becomes one with the luminously smiling mouth, to the impressionistic *Man Reading* (1894).

ROOM 30

This room contains exemplary works of early twentieth century Tuscan culture. Next to two "Impressionistic" paintings, *Chickens* and *Portrait of the Artist's Wife* (c 1913) by Armando Spadini is the large and famous *Confidences* (c 1919-1922) in which the domestic theme of the intimate conversation between a girl and her mother becomes monumentally classic, typical of post-World War I Tuscan art. The different shades of white in the clothing and bed linens are broken by reminders of the art and culture of days gone by – the work basket, the sixteenth century "Annunciation" – and the contemporary works of Matisse and Bonnard as suggested by the red swirls on the violet tablecloth at a daringly two dimensional angle.

On the same wall: *Flowers* by Mario Puccini, the self-taught painter from Livorno who spent the first decade of the century in France, and the elegant still-lifes by Galileo Chini, Fillide Levasti and mainly Oscar Ghiglia in whose painting the thick magnolia leaves and the geometric roundness of the oranges stand out, without shadows, on the white tablecloth, a

Faith, by *Galileo Chini* (Room 28).

fine example of formal study emphasized by the overturned perspective. Then there are landscapes in the style of Cézanne by Arturo Cecchi and Alfredo Müller and a good selection of sculptures by Boncinelli and Moschi along with some plaster models by Domenico Trentacoste, including the smiling face of a girl and a *Mother*. Flanking the doors are paintings by Giovanni Costetti illustrating the artist's intellectual curiosity and hence the variety of his subjects and forms of expression. Two walls are entirely dedicated to paintings by Elizabeth Chaplin, the artist who lived most of her life in Fiesole and bequeathed many works to the Gallery. The exhibit comprises paintings from before World War I showing her lively interests and the impact that international culture had on her work, from the *Family Portrait* (1906) an obvious echo of poetry by Maurice Denis to the Secessionist air of the *Study Hour* (1911) and *Nenette Going Up the Stairs* (c 1912). Gaugin's influence can be seen in the beautiful portrait *Brother Soldier* and the *Shepherd's Daughters*, and hints of Matisse are evident in *Nenette with the Cage*. Elizabeth Chaplin's individualism and intimate poetry are widely reflected in these works.

The items in this room will be moved to the mezzanine which is being remodelled to house the Twentieth Century Art Collections. The paintings and statues will be arranged to illustrate the the many facets of the Florentine cultural climate between the two World Wars. The groupings will represent both the figurative movements and the intellectual trends of the individual artists in a manner that will also and inevitably take chronology into account. From the Post-Impressionistic experiences of Libero Andreotti, Antony de Witt or Alimondo Ciampi to those of the artists who, in the twenties, joined the "Novecento" group founded by Margherita Sarfatti: Arturo Tosi, Virgilio Guidi, Ferruccio Ferrazzi. Next come the artists who, urged on by Raffaello Franchi, participated in the "Novecento Toscano", first Felice Carena, Baccio Maria Bacci, Guido Ferroni and then Primo Conti, Giannino Marchig, Giovanni Colacicchi, Arturo Selva, Italo Griselli and Romano Romanelli. In parallel, the artists linked to the

Peace and *Indolence*, by *Galileo Chini* (Room 28).

First Birthday, by *Plinio Nomellini* (Room 29).

"Selvaggio" group (the magazine founded by Mino Maccari): Ardengo Soffici, Ottone Rosai and Maccari himself.

Tuscan art in the 'thirties will be represented by portraits by Bacchelli, Mannucci, Zuccoli; city views and landscapes by Fillide Levasti, Silvio Polloni, Mario Marcucci, and Dino Bausi; still-lifes by Onofrio Martinelli and by artists who though less-known are exemplary of that cultural moment such as Umberto Benedetti. The sculptors include Carlo Rivalta, Agostino Giovannini, Bruno Innocenti, Raffaello Salimbeni and Oscar Gallo.

Along with the paintings and statues by the these Tuscan artists, the exhibits will extend to artworks acquired by the Gallery of Modern Art at the major international shows, mainly the ones held every two years in Venice and every four years in Rome. Some of the artists to keep in mind are: Mario Cavaglieri, Antonio Donghi, Giuseppe Capogrossi, Francesco Messina; and then Carlo Carrà, Giorgio De Chirico, Alberto Savinio, Gino Severini and Filippo De Pisis, who all exhibited their works together at the 1932 Biennial in Venice in the section "Italians in Paris".

THE WINTER APARTMENTS

This portion of the palace, built to designs by Bartolomeo Ammannati, was completed between 1580 and 1590 and was immediately handed over to Maria de'Medici, future queen of France. After she left Florence, her step-brother Don Antonio lived there until 1658 when the rooms were already documented as the "Gallery of His Serene Highness Prince Leopoldo" who gathered books, manuscripts, mathematical instruments, sculptures, drawings and paintings there. At the time, the walls were hung with fine tapestries in brilliant tones that were later replaced by crimson fabric when the apartments were taken over by Cardinal Francesco Maria, Leopoldo's nephew.

Neither the Regency nor the early years of Lorraine rule brought about any major changes in this part of the palace which was first used by the archdukes Francis and Ferdinand of Hapsburg-Lorraine, and after 1775 by the archduchesses. It was only after 1792 when Ferdinand III chose them as his Winter Apartments that the first changes would be made by Maria Gaspare Paoletti, and the painters Giuseppe Terreni and Luigi Catani. Most of the decorations on the walls, ceilings and doors date from this period. After the Napoleonic interlude, work was resumed around 1815, under the direction of Pasquale Poccianti who completed the Grooms' Antechamber (Sala degli Staffieri) and the majestic ballroom, where the stucco works pick up the neoclassical themes of the White Room. Used by the dowager grand duchess Maria Ferdinanda during the Restoration when the Savoy monarchs came to Florence, the entire suite became the residence of the Kings of Italy (1865-1911) and later of the duchess of Aosta.

The apartments contain some curious mid-nineteenth century pieces purchased by Vittorio Emanuele II at the Exhibition of 1861 as well as countless decorative items (vases, china, glass, desksets, clocks and gilded bronzes). The large number of paintings focus on Savoy subjects.

The Grooms' Room

This room was decorated between 1819 and 1824 to plans by Pasquale Poccianti. Not only did the architect design the ceiling and wall decorations, he also designed the mahogany piece with gilded bronzes, made by the Florentine cabinet-maker, Giuseppe Colzi, and set into the wall facing the window. The *Apollo and Daphne* on the ceiling was frescoed by Luigi Catani of Prato.

The Yellow Sitting Room.

Antechamber

The nineteenth century temperas that adorn the walls and ceiling were probably executed by Giorgio Berti, while the roundel with dancing putti in the middle of the ceiling was painted by Antonio Marini.

Ballroom

This fine room with its neoclassical stucco work was built to plans by Poccianti during the early years of the Lorraine Restoration.

Dining Room

It was Gaspare Maria Paoletti, court architect, who drew up the plans for this room that was built in 1795 and was originally supposed to be a music room. This explains the decorations by Terreni which were inspired by the mythological origins and historical evolution of music.

Yellow Sitting Room

The neoclassical ceiling decorations can be attributed to Terreni. The mid-nineteenth century furniture was made in Florence while the monumental chandelier was constructed in the XVIII century with Viennese crystals. A late Empire style clock stands on the mantle.
One of the noteworthy paintings in the room is the *Alpine Landscape: Valley of Gressoney* by Giuseppe Camino (b. Turin 1818-d. 1890, Caluso).

Red Sitting Room

Like the Yellow Room here, too, the decorations are neoclassical temperas. Some of the furniture was made by local craftsmen in an exuberant Neobaroque style. The marble-topped console was carved by Angiolo Barbetti in 1856 while the monumental mirror was made in the Levera brothers' workshop around 1861. The firescreen (made in Parma around 1750), the armchairs and "canapé" are all eighteenth century.
A painting by Arturo Calosci, *Winter*, hangs on the right wall.

Study

A small passageway connects the Red Sitting Room and the Queen's Study; here, too, the tempera decorations can be attributed to Terreni. Facing the fireplace there is a lacquered two-part drop-leaf mid-eighteenth century piece from England and a round table with a green Egyptian porphyry top dated 1816.

The room contains several paintings including *The Ruins of the Temple of Segesta* by Giovanni Cobianchi next to the fireplace, and a Roman mosaic depicting the *Colosseum* near the door.

Dressing Room

The room has a coffered ceiling decorated around 1821; the chest between the two windows by Giuseppe Colzi and Andrea Fondelli, who worked in bronze, is also from the same period. The two late-eighteenth century *armoires* were painted by Giuseppe Maria Terreni and Luigi Catani. The wood dresser with brass and tortoise shell inlays was purchased in Florence in 1856; the cheval-glass made the same year is by the Florentine cabinet-makers Chalon et Estienne.

Bedroom

Terreni's tempera decorations on the ceiling and doors dating from around 1792 are still intact. The pair of semi-circular chests was made by Giuseppe Colzi in 1821 as was the two-part piece that was delivered to the Pitti Palace in 1853. The holy water stoup, next to the prie-dieu with the Nativity and the "Second Empire" medal case, are from Parma. The bed was made for the dukes of Lucca sometime around 1820. The clock on top of the chest was made in Paris and can be dated around the late seventeenth century. The painting above the bed, *Rest During the Flight into Egypt*, is by A. Domenico Gabbiani; the painting on the side wall is by an unknown late seventeenth century Venetian artist.

Wardrobe and Boudoir

From the bedroom the queen could go directly to the wardrobe and then to the boudoir. Both rooms were decorated towards the end of the eighteenth century; there are two interesting consoles with *scagliola* tops made around 1798.

The King's Bedroom

The suite consisting of a sofa, four armchairs and several chairs was made by Carlo Toussaint who carved them specifically for this room between 1794 and 1796. The "canapé" bed is probably French and made in the early nineteenth century. The round table with the geometric-inlay white marble top was most likely made by G.B. Youf around 1823.
The copy of Raphael's *Madonna of the Chair* above the bed dates from the XIX century.

The King's Bedroom.

Study

One of the most noteworthy pieces in this room is the secretary with 12 columns and mirrors from Parma, made in the eighteen thirties, and the semi-precious stone cabinet made by Enrico Bosi of the Opificio Fiorentino in 1861. The portrait of *Umberto I* above the sofa is by the Neapolitan artist Eurisio Capocci.

Red Room

Antonio Luzzi's ceiling fresco of *Minerva Enthroned* dates from just before 1815. The two eighteenth century consoles with antique red velvet tops are from the Throne Room in the Ducal Palace in Parma while the set of two porcelain candelabra and clock on the mantle are Second Empire French.

Chinese Sitting Room

This, one of the most quaint and exotic rooms, was created for the Grand Duchess Maria Ferdinanda in 1842. The chandelier is decorated with Chinese mandarins and dragons; then there is a curious gilded bronze pagoda-shaped clock with "pâte de verre" decorations and two lacquer chests with mother-of-pearl and gilded bronze ornaments that were made in France during the mid-eighteenth century and then modified in Florence. On the walls are temperas by Terreni (1739-1811) depicting various Florentine celebrations and some Bourbon portraits by Anton Raphael Mengs (1728-1779).

Palazzina della Meridiana.

THE COSTUME GALLERY

The Costume Gallery, opened in 1983, occupies part of the Palazzina della Meridiana which is actually an extension of the palace's south wing. It gets its name from the sundial (*meridiana* in Italian) in the vestibule outside the Grand Duke Ferdinand's apartments. Originally it was an open loggia; the ceiling fresco, *Allegory of Time and the Arts* (1692-1693) is by Anton Domenico Gabbiani. Work on the building was begun under the reign of Peter Leopold in 1776 by Gaspare Maria Paoletti who worked on it until 1813, with help from Giuseppe Cacialli, and built the "lions' staircase", the six rooms in the western part and the main façade overlooking the Boboli Gardens. Between 1822 and 1840 it was enlarged by Pasquale Poccianti who built the southern façade and added the ballroom and adjacent rooms expanding it towards the Botanical Garden and the Specola. Poccianti also supervised the fresco decorations of the rooms between 1833 and 1837 as well as the stucco work in the ballroom and the overall furnishing of the new building.

Members of the Lorraine family lived in the Meridiana until the French invasion of 1799, later it was home to the Regent of Etruria, Maria Luisa of Bourbon Parma (1803-1807), Elisa Baciocchi (1807-1814), again the Lorraines when Ferdinand III returned from exile and finally the House of Savoy from 1862 until the monarchy was abolished in 1946. The furnishings and wall hangings were completely renovated in 1810 for Elisa Baciocchi and again between 1862 and 1865 when the capital of Italy was moved to Florence and King Vittorio Emanuele II chose it as his home; Umberto I and Queen Margherita also lived in the Meridiana while in Florence. The six state rooms were decorated with rich silks; the furniture came from Lucca, Parma and Piacenza; the ceiling frescoes made way for new murals. The current decor reflects the last Savoy period at the beginning of this century when the Meridiana was inhabited by the Count of Turin and the Prince and Princess of Piedmont, Umberto and Maria Josè who ordered further renovations.

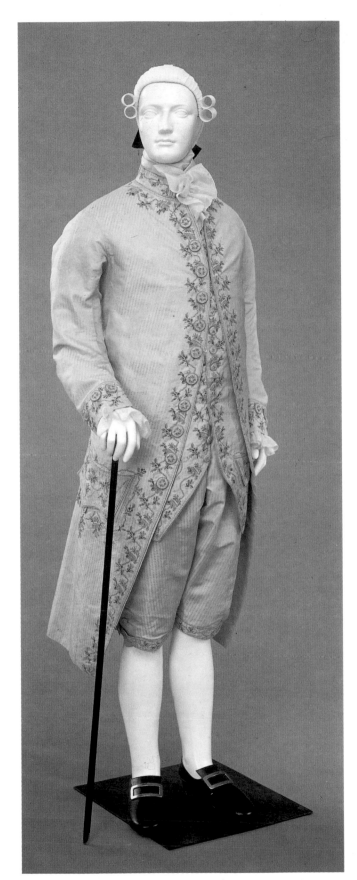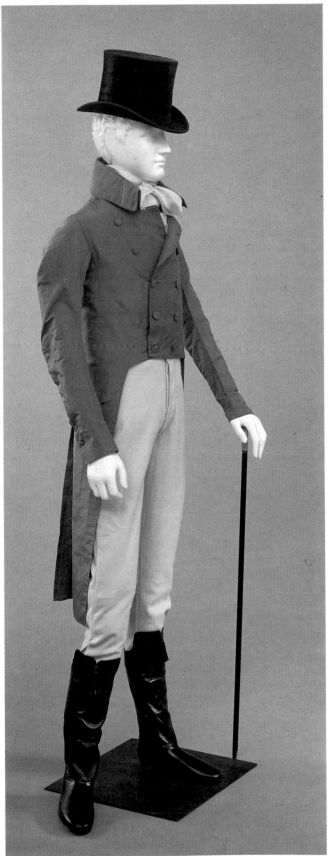

XVIII century Italian-made three quarter coat; right: Redingote, Italian (?), late XVIII early XIX century.

Top left: "Robe à la française", 1770-75 ca., French (?); above: early XIX century Italian (?) ballgown; opposite: French (?) styling, 1826-28.

The Costume Gallery occupies thirteen rooms including six over the façade. They contain historic items of clothing from the early eighteenth century to about nineteen twenty-five selected to illustrate changes in fabrics and fashions through the years. The costumes, almost all of which were donated by individuals and institutions are shown in special temperature-controlled display cases for two to three years and then are replaced by others from the same period. This "rotation" helps preserve the garments from prolonged stress due to exposure and "wear". Items in need of repair or that have been modified with respect to their original styling and cut are restored at the Textile Restoration Laboratory adjoining the Costume Gallery. Women's clothing predominates since men's garments, subject to more wear and tear, are harder to acquire.

Italian garment, 1840-45 ca..

From room *V* to room *VIII* we see further changes up to the last decade of the nineteenth century: crinolines, hoop-skirts and whalebone corsets and necklines that became more modest. In the eighteensixties styles changed again, skirts were gathered in the back and fell straight in front. In the 'seventies and 'eighties fashions could be described as vertical, with fitted bodices and skirts that were drawn back creating the "tapisserie" look with the famous bustles. There are several examples of this style in rooms *IX* and *X* with fashions from the 'nineties leading into room *XI* and this century. Now dresses were simpler and simpler until the 'twenties: hemlines went up, the lines were agile, hair was cut "à la garçonne" and a real fashion revolution took place that is continuing even today.

The rooms in the Meridiana also house fine examples of Tuscan Romantic art with works by painters and sculptors who trained at the Accademia delle Belle Arti. In addition the wall hangings and furniture are also of museum quality.

Ballgown, Italian (?), 1869 ca..

Afternoon attire, Italian, 1880-82 ca..

The costumes are arranged more or less in the following order: the first two rooms (*I* and *II*) are dedicated to eighteenth century clothing. In the men's garments we can observe the transition from the long, square-cut tailcoats with ample cuffs with the long just-au-corps with sleeves, to the more tapered tail-coat with straight collar and sleeveless waistcoat, and of course, knee-length breeches. Eighteenth century women's dresses were distinguished by elaborate overgarments with fitted bodices and low necklines with pleats starting from the shoulders, elbow length sleeves and skirts with either a single center "panier" or with two on the sides: this was the typical "robe à la française".

Rooms *III* and *IV* contain costumes from the beginning and first half of the XIX century. Note the subdued neoclassical taste in the tubular dresses with short trains, high waist and puffed sleeves in soft colors. These were followed by the Restoration style with shorter, slighter fuller skirts, the waistlines dropped slightly and "gigot" sleeves with high cuffs came into fashion.

Italian fashions, early XX century.

French-made dress 1905-06.

Room I, formerly the grooms' room, is decorated with red silk moiré (1905). The most noteworthy items of furniture include two "boulle" desks (one is an XVIII century original). *Room II*: neoclassical green damask wall decorations (dating from 1907); the paintings are from the XVIII century and the mosaic table, signed by Montecucchi (1804) is on a carved and gilded late eighteenth century base. *Room III*: crimson and ivory fabric from the Savoy period (1864) covers the walls; part of the furniture is contemporary. The murals by the Florentine painter Annibale Gatti, who worked from 1860 on, portray *Italia risorta presentata al Congresso delle Nazioni dal genio di Casa Savoia* (1861). The ballroom and the room on the right are used for special costume exhibitions; the stucco bas-reliefs depicting Dionysian scenes were made by the sculptors Luigi Pampaloni, Aristodemo Costoli, Emilio Santarelli and Ulisse Cambi (1831 ca.).

Room IV: the ceiling paintings by Giorgio Berti, a rather neoclassical academic painter of scenes, shows *Dante, Florentine Ambassador to Pope Boniface VIII* (1860 ca).

Room V: Francesco Nenci, known for historical and religious paintings in addition to portraits, decorated the walls with the *Banquet in the House of Alcinoos* (1833); the nineteenth century neo-Gothic display cases contain porcelain from different factories (1820-1855). *Room VI*: the *Pazzi Plot*, the subject of the ceiling fresco by Cesare Mussini, considered one of the greatest Tuscan romantic painters, is based on Alfieri's play (1861). The painting by Angiolo Fabbrici is entitled *Lorenzo de' Medici seeks refuge from the plotters in the Sacristy surrounded by Poliziano and other friends* (1858 ca.).

Room VII: Antonio Marini, a purist painter and restorer of frescoes painted the murals on the four lunettes, *Episodes from the Life of Torquato Tasso*, which were completed after his death by Pietro Pezzati (1860-61). The gouaches by Saverio della Gatta show scenes in traditional Neapolitan costumes (1820-21). *Room VIII*: here we see two lunettes with *Scenes from the Life of Michelangelo* (1861 ca.) by Annibale Gatti and a drop-leaf chest with a gilded mirror made in Italy sometime around 1850.

We go through the passageway on the left, via room III to reach *Room IX*: the draperies and wall hangings in green silk brocade date from 1864; the murals by Cesare Mussini depict *Italy Crowning the Arts (1862)*.

Room X: red silk moiré adorns the walls (1864); Vittorio Emanuele bought most of the furniture at the 1861 Exposition. The ceiling painting of *Cornelia and the Matron of Capua* was done by Ferdinando Folchi and Antonio Marini. *Room XI*: the blue and gold silk on the walls was purchased in Lyon in 1833 and installed in 1864. The ceiling painting of *Solomon's Dream and Scenes from His Life* by Luigi Sabatelli and Ferdinando Folchi is the only painting that remains from the Bourbon-Parma period. The painting, *The Bentivoglio Mercenaries Insult Savonarola in His Cell* (1867) is by Federico Andreotti.

Formal attire, Florentine-made, 1923 ca..

Ceremonial coach that belonged to Ferdinand III of Lorraine.

THE CARRIAGE MUSEUM

Housed in the Southern Rondò of the palace, the museum contains carriages used by the Lorraine and Savoy courts. In the entrance room a series of watercolors by Stanislao Grimaldi (1825-1903) depict horses from the royal stables, two of which had been ridden by Vittorio Emanuele II who also owned the paintings.

Highlights of the collection are three luxurious covered carriages Ferdinand III of Lorraine ordered upon his return from exile in 1818 to refresh the fleet of ceremonial vehicles. Period documents tell us that the work was divided among craftsmen from various fields: the saddlers Busi and Dani were in charge of the project and they called in Cioci and Gori bronze workers; Paolo Sani, engraver; Antonio Marini, painter and all the other artisans painters, gilders, box-makers, smiths, spinet-makers and upholsterers. The grand duke's carriage, made in 1818, is probably the most lavish: with gold decorations, the imaginatively crafted structural elements such as the springs shaped like winged dragons and the sumptuous upholstery. Antonio Marini's paintings on gold decorate the body: triumphant teams of four with Lorenzo the Magnificent and Poliziano, Cosimo I and Vasari, Cosimo II and Galileo and finally Ferdinand III alone, surrounded by cherubs bearing symbols of abundance and trade to symbolize the continuity between the Medici and Lorraine lines.

This carriage was recently restored. The other two which were part of the grand duke's retinue date from

1819 and 1820. They are structurally similar to the first, but the decorative work is not as lavish. The bodies are decorated with gold on a dark blue background; on one we can see the nine Muses and three Graces, while the other is adorned by the Virtues. The sedan chair dates from a few years later (1822): Ferdinand III ordered it made to carry the wife of Crown Prince Leopold from the Meridiana to the Baptistry for the christening of their first child, Maria Carolina. An even older one, documented 1793 and that is before the grand duke's exile, was ordered by Ferdinand III for his wife, the Grand Duchess Marie Louise de Bourbon of Spain.

The coach that belonged to Ferdinando II, king of Naples in the early nineteenth century and brought to Florence by the Savoy rulers is particularly impressive. Silver reliefs depicting allegories of Naples and Palermo were mounted on the gilded copper body, and the Savoy arms were put on the doors to replace the Bourbon symbols. It may be that the ceremonial carriage from the late XVIII-early XIX century from the royal stables of the House of Savoy had once belonged to Francesco IV, duke of Modena; it is decorated with mythological scenes on a gold ground. The oldest coach in the collection is an elegant Rococo (1730-1750) coupé for the city which must have belonged to some noble family given its refined elegance. Part of the leather covered body is decorated with scenes of the four seasons.

Detail of the luxurious ceremonial coach.

THE PORCELAIN MUSEUM

The Porcelain Museum, in the Casino del Cavaliere, at the top of the Boboli Gardens, against the bastions was opened in 1973. The original building was used by Cardinal Leopoldo de' Medici to receive artists and men of letters. The secluded place was also a favorite of Cosimo III who had it converted into a little palace around 1700 for his son Gian Gastone, where he took his French and science lessons. During the Lorraine period it was rebuilt in its current form by the architect Giuseppe Del Rosso and was used by the court for summertime festivities and celebrations. In front of the building is a rose garden with a pool. The bronze "Monkey Fountain", traditionally attributed to Pietro Tacca with a puttino reputedly by Pierino da Vinci was removed for reasons of conservation.

The museum today houses what was left of the porcelains after the Savoy court moved to Rome and the collections sold. The porcelain all belonged to the various dynasties that had lived in the Pitti Palace over the centuries: Medici, Lorraine, French, Bourbon-Parma and Savoy.

The *first room*, with an eighteenth century Murano glass chandelier from the palace was once a ballroom.

Today it contains *French and Italian porcelain*. To the left of the entrance is the section dedicated to the *Real Fabbrica di Capodimonte* in Naples. Many of the pieces from this factory were gifts of Neapolitan sovereigns with dynastic bonds to the Lorraine grand dukes. Peter Leopold's sister, Maria Carolina had, in fact, married Ferdinando IV of Naples; Ferdinand III, Peter Leopold's son, became Emperor of Austria in 1790 and married Maria Luisa, daughter of Ferdinando IV the same year. Gifts of porcelain from Naples were made during royal visits to Florence. The royal factory was revived by Ferdinando IV in 1771. Under the management of Domenico Venuti (1779-1800), a Tuscan interested in archeological treasures, the factory began copying ancient models, reawakening an interest in antiquities: these were the years that the excavations at Herculaneum and Pompei and the great Roman monuments were compulsory stops on every Grand Tour. Filippo Tagliolini, a sculptor who had already worked in Vienna, joined Venuti and dedicated his efforts mainly to "biscuit" china. In 1807 the government established by Napoleon entrusted the factory to Giovanni Poulard Prad who managed it until 1820 and exerted a definite

The Bear School, attributed to *Filippo Tagliolini, Real Fabbrica di Napoli.*

Cup and saucer, *Naples, Manifattura di Giovanni Pou-lard Prad;* opposite: creamer, *Real Fabbrica di Napoli;* below, right: *"Donna di Ducenta"*, attributed to *Filippo Tagliolini, Real Fabbrica di Napoli.*

French influence on its products.

In the classic vein we can see biscuit figurines of historical and mythological subjects, Tagliolini's copies of pieces excavated at Herculaneum, and a series of biscuit busts of famous characters from antiquity (philosophers, adventurers, poets and divinities) copied from marble and bronze busts which are displayed in the Museo Archeologico in Naples.

A group of eighteen biscuit figurines by Filippo Taglioni portrays costumes from the Kingdom of Naples. They are based on gouaches showing costumes of the realm that Ferdinando IV had ordered from Alessandro d'Anna and Saverio della Gatta (who was replaced by Antonio Berotti); the paintings were done in 1783 after a preliminary observation tour. The group, which is mounted on a pyramid, was supposed to have been the centerpiece of a porcelain table service decorated with the costumes the Realm based on the gouache paintings. The statuettes were sent to Florence in 1785 along with a series on the same subject, perhaps on the occasion of a visit by Ferdinando IV and his wife. The two "déjeuners" are also linked to the revival of interest in antiquities: one is decorated with Egyptian motifs and the other in the "Etruscan" style (1790-1800 ca). The English clay "déjeuner" with the arms of the grand duke Peter Leopold and Maria Luisa of Bourbon Spain on a black background may have been a gift to the grand dukes from the Neapolitan rulers in 1785. The same may be true for the biscuit group, known as the "The Bear School," attributed to Tagliolini and part of another characteristic theme of the factory: the comical or burlesque.

The cup with the portrait of Caroline Bonaparte, wife of Jacques Murat, king of Naples (1808-1815) came from Giovanni Poulard Prad's factory (1810 ca.). Biscuit cups with portraits are typical of the Napoleonic period.

Above, from the left, two pieces from *the Ginori factory:* Turkish Woman and Sherbert dish; below:
pitcher and vase, *Vincennes Factory.*

Sugar bowl and tray, from Elisa Baciocchi's dinner service, *Sèvres factory.*

The *Manifattura di Doccia*, founded by the Ginori family, worked consistently for the grand dukes. It was expanded through Peter Leopold's policies which set up a proper business relationship for the supply of "dinner sets for daily use", decorated with bouquets or tulips. Orders continued to be placed by the Bourbon-Parma family and Elisa Baciocchi. When Ferdinand III returned from his exile, he too, bought a great deal of Ginori porcelain. When Florence was capital of Italy many pieces of porcelain from Doccia and other factories were included among the art objects the Savoy monarchs brought to Pitti from Parma--several of which had belonged to Marie Louise of Austria. The Ginori factory continued to supply the royal household at Palazzo Pitti with porcelain even after the capital was transferred to Rome.

Left wall: the initial period of activity under Carlo Ginori (1737-1757) is documented by a group of pieces purchased at the auction of the Villoresi collection in 1935. It consists of white porcelain "versions" of metal objects or items decorated in the manner of antique white and blue Florentine pottery, types that were made through the years and here are represented up to about 1780. The next display case contains two figurines of Turkish women (1745-1750), typical of the factory's early days, inspired by Jacopo Ligozzi's temperas, and brought from Parma. Typical examples of the Rococo style made under the direction of Lorenzo Ginori (1758-1791) are the consommé cup with raised decorations, inspired by Meissen porcelain (1770 ca.) and a set of sherbet cups (1770-1780 ca). There are also interesting reproductions of pieces from other European factories the Ginori's had toured to learn how to replace broken pieces (1770-1850). One of these is a "déjeuner" that had belonged to Marie Louise of Austria, and brought from Parma: the inspiration was Sèvres (1815-1825 ca.), and two plates that are copies of Japanese Arita porcelain (1840). The showcase on the entrance wall is dedicated to dinner sets with floral motifs ordered by the Lorraines for everyday use (1750-1780) the bouquets and especially the tulips were inspired by Chinese "famille rose" porcelain.

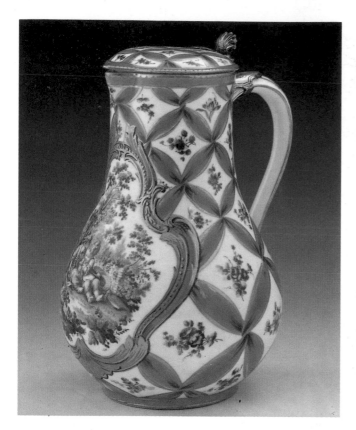

Two pieces from *Sèvres;* from the left: **pitcher** and **oyster stand**.

Most of the *French porcelain* comes from Parma. Louise Elizabeth de Bourbon, daughter of Louis XV king of France and wife of Pilippe de Bourbon (1739-1765) had brought an enormous quantity of French porcelain to Parma. Some of the services have been lost; others are in the Quirinale Palace in Rome, and others still are in the Pitti Palace. The late eighteenth-early nineteenth century Sèvres porcelain pieces were mostly gifts from Napoleon to the king of Etruria, to Elisa Baciocchi and to Ferdinand III of Lorraine when he was exiled from Florence (1799-1814).

The case on the opposite wall contains pieces from the *Vincennes factory* established in 1740. The factory obtained the official protection of Louis XV in 1753 and in 1756 was moved to *Sèvres* and for three years was the personal property of the king. Vincennes and Sèvres porcelain is characterized by a dominant color. The oldest is blue in various shades. The lapislazuli tone dates from about 1750-1770; pink, green and light blue come from Vincennes and early Sèvres. Examples of the dark blue Vincennes style with white centers and golden birds and vines (1753 and 1754) can be seen in some of the pieces from the dinner sets; the Rococo style pitcher and tray with a turquoise background (1756 and 1754) are also from Vincennes. On the same wall two other displays are dedicated to Sèvres porcelain: a large vase in "bleu lapis caillouté" with scenes from Boucher's prints in the white medallions (1757). The winding ribbons that decorate a pitcher include another typical color, "Pompadour pink" (1757). The groups of biscuit

figurines were used to decorate tables (1800-1850). To the right of the entrance two more showcases are dedicated to Sèvres. The items include pieces from two table services decorated with bouquets (1765-1769) and four exceptional and indeed unique oyster stands consisting of 18 shell-shaped plates with blue edges and bouquets (1759) from Parma. The two middle displays contain Elisa Baciocchi's dinner sets made at Sèvres between 1809 and 1810 that she received from Napoleon after he had given her the Grand Duchy of Tuscany. The set consists of two parts. The "entrée" service is decorated with gold flowers and dark blue trim on a white background; the "dessert" service has blue festoons alternating with gold medallions and medallions with symbolic figures.

On the right hand wall the display case contains parts of a service from *Chantilly* (1760 ca.) the factory which was founded in 1726 and lasted until 1800. These items came to Florence via Parma; the showcase also contains some biscuit groups from the Tournai factory (1762-1781). Above the mantle there is a porcelain portrait of Napoleon (1810) based on a painting by François Gerard which Napoleon himself had presented to Ferdinand III. While he was in exile the grand duke attended the wedding of Napoleon and Marie Louise, Ferdinand's niece. The grand duke was officially representing his brother, Emperor of Austria on this occasion and did so again at the baptism of Napoleon's son, the king of Rome. On both occasions he received porcelain gifts from Napoleon: this portrait was presented at the

Vase, *Sèvres factory;* below: sugar bowl, *Meissen.*

Three figures entitled "the discovered lover", *Meissen.*

christening. Left of the mantle are specimens from other *Parisian factories: Locré, Dagoty, Dihl and Guerard* and *Denuelle* which, with the exception of Denuelle, flourished at the end of the eighteenth century. Denuelle was founded in 1819 and in 1823 took over Dagoty. The nut-colored coffee set with gold decorations and medallions with miniature landscapes (1810 ca.) and part of a dessert set consisting of white plates with a green band and stylized gold trim with various figures ranging from landscapes to ancient forms and animals (1810 ca.) are from Dagoty. The white dessert, tea and coffee service with the dark blue edges and gold decoration (1830 ca.-1835) is from Denuelle.

Room II, Viennese porcelain. This is the largest collection of Viennese porcelain outside the Austrian capital; it came to the Pitti Palace via the Lorraine grand dukes, the younger branch of the Hapsburg-Lorraine dynasty. Most pieces, including the breakfast set and cups, were collected by Ferdinand III during his Viennese exile (1799-1814). It seems that he himself selected fine quality pieces of which significant examples have been preserved. A covered bowl (1725-37) represents the

factory's oldest period; after Meissen, under the management of Du Paquier (1718-1744) it was the second factory to make hard-clay porcelain. In 1744 the factory came under state ownership and for forty years specialized in biscuit figurines and groups that we see here, as well as painted porcelain dinner sets in the Rococo style. The porcelain from the following period, Sorgenthal (1784-1805) is characterized by dinner and breakfast sets and cups in the neoclassical style with extremely refined colors, decorations and gilding. The most interesting items from the last period were made under the management of Matthias Niedermayer (1805-1827). Beginning on the right: we see porcelain from the first period and a breakfast set with a "blu caillouté" background (1765-1775) with the initials ML, perhaps a wedding gift to Maria Luisa of Spain who married Peter Leopold. Next come Viennese pieces made between 1780 and 1800, including biscuit statuettes: note the figurines of Maria Theresa and Joseph II attributed to Anton Grassi (1778-1780) and coffee set with "trompe l'oeil" wood decorations, typical of German porcelain from that period. On the back wall, the display cases

Vase in the Chinese style, *Meissen*.

contain interesting examples of Viennese cups from the late XVIII/early XIX centuries. On the left, there are various types of breakfast sets, some of which are decorated with landscapes. Note the pure neoclassical style set with Viennese scenes (1800 ca.) and another with a picture of the first steel bridge built in Europe at Coalbrook Dale on the tray (1779). Two miniature sets (1795-1800) belonged to the daughters of Ferdinand III, and a dresser set with black silhouette portraits of members of the imperial family dates from about 1800. There is an unusual breakfast set that belonged to Ferdinand III (1810-1813): the scene on the tray tells the story of the Vestal Virgins' escape from the Gauls, and it was interpreted as a reference to the grand duke's exile from Florence. On the right wall, there is a coffee set from the Würzburg factory (1808-1814): the tray is decorated with an allegory honoring Ferdinand III of Lorraine portrayed in the bust on a column. The middle display case contains the grand Viennese dinner set decorated with bouquets, and blue ribbons in the Rococo style inspired by models from Sèvres (1770-1780), and biscuit statuettes used for table decorations. *Room III* contains *porcelain from Meissen and other factories*. Meissen was the first factory which, established in 1710 under the patronage of Augustus the

Maria Teresa, biscuit sculpture by *Anton Grassi (Vienna)* below: cooler, cup and tray from the "grand Vienna service", *Vienna Factory.*

Soup tureen, Chinese inspiration, from the *Meissen factory*.

Strong, elector of Saxony, produced hard-clay porcelain. During the first half of the century both shapes and patterns were based on Chinese porcelain. Famous painters worked for Meissen, including Johann Gregor Höroldt (1696-1775), as did the sculptors of figurines that were so suited to the elegant and subtle eighteenth century tastes. The most creative and widely copied of these masters was Johann Joachim Kändler (1706-1775). While many of the pieces here come from the Parma collection of Marie Louise of Austria, many of the older items had belonged to Gian Gastone de'Medici. On the right is a white and blue set with gold edges in a Chinese mode (1725-1740) followed by graceful items from the early period at Meissen decorated by painters from Augsburg. The motifs are naturalistic or Chinese, like the two unusual tankards (1725-30). The central showcase contains a teapot and cups with Oriental subjects (1723-26) and three rare pieces: two tortoise shaped sugar bowls and a hen-shaped teapot (1720-1735) that had also belonged to Gian Gastone. On the opposite wall, parts of a set and painted porcelain figurines from Meissen and the samples of the large dinner set in the middle of the room are from a later period in the Meissen factory's long history. The case against the entrance wall contains porcelain from other factories: pieces from two large services from Berlin (1770 ca.) from the Parma collection, cups from the Nymphenburg factory and three large biscuit peices from Frankenthal, all of which had been royal factories. And finally there are two examples of English china: a yellow, soft-clay set with red flowers and a few pieces from Worcester.

REFERENCES

1960
MORANDINI F., *Mostra documentaria e iconografica di Palazzo Pitti e Giardino di Boboli*, Firenze

1968
ASCHENGREEN PIACENTI K., *Il Museo degli Argenti*, Milano

1971
DEL BRAVO C., *Disegni italiani del XIX secolo*, catalogo della mostra, Firenze

1972
Cultura neoclassica e romantica nella Toscana granducale, catalogo della mostra a cura di S. PINTO, Firenze

1973
ERIKSEN S., *Le porcellane francesi a Palazzo Pitti*, Firenze

1974
HEIKAMP D., *Il tesoro di Lorenzo il Magnifico, i vasi*, Firenze
TABAKOFF S.K., *The European Porcelain in Palazzo Pitti*, "Keramos", 65, pp. 3-15.

1975
DEL BRAVO C., *Milleottocentosessanta*, "Annali della Scuola Normale Superiore di Pisa", III, V, pp. 779-795

1977
ASCHENGREEN PIACENTI K., *The Summer Apartment of the Grand Dukes*, "Apollo", CVI, pp. 190-197.
Rubens e la pittura fiamminga del Seicento nelle collezioni pubbliche fiorentine, catalogo della mostra a cura di D. BODART, Firenze

1978
Tiziano nelle Gallerie fiorentine, catalogo della mostra, Firenze

1979
Curiosità di una reggia. Vicende della Guardaroba di Palazzo Pitti, catalogo della mostra, Firenze

1980
Palazzo Vecchio: committenza e collezionismo medicei, catalogo della mostra, Firenze 1980

1982
CANEVA C., *Il Giardino di Boboli*, Firenze
La Galleria Palatina. Storia della quadreria granducale di Palazzo Pitti, catalogo della mostra a cura di M. MOSCO, Firenze

1983
CLARKE T. - D'AGLIANO A. - TABAKOFF S.K., *Porcellane dell'800 a Palazzo Pitti*, catalogo della mostra, Firenze

1983
RAGUSI L., Schede ministeriali relative al Museo delle Carrozze

1983-1990
La Galleria del Costume / 1-4, Firenze, 1983, 1986, 1988, 1990

1984
Raffaello a Firenze, catalogo della mostra, Milano

1985
SPALLETTI E., *Gli anni del Caffè Michelangelo*, Roma

1986
Andrea del Sarto 1486-1530, catalogo della mostra, Firenze
D'AGLIANO A., *Le porcellane italiane a Palazzo Pitti*, Firenze
SISI C., *Disegni dell'Ottocento della Collezione Batelli*, catalogo della mostra, Firenze

1988
I gioielli dell'Elettrice Palatina al Museo degli Argenti, Firenze
Palazzo Pitti, a cura di M. CHIARINI, testi di M. CHIARINI, K. ASCHENGREEN PIACENTI, E. SPALLETTI, Firenze

1989
Ottocento e Novecento. Acquisizioni 1974-1989, catalogo della mostra a cura di E. SPALLETTI - C. SISI, Firenze

1990
ASCHENGREEN PIACENTI K., *Museo degli Argenti*, Firenze
PADOVANI S., *Galleria Palatina*, Firenze
Pietro Paolo Rubens, catalogo della mostra a cura di D. BODART, Roma
Tiziano, catalogo della mostra, Venezia

1991
Boboli '90, Atti del Convegno Internazionale, Firenze
COLLE E., *Palazzo Pitti. Il Quartiere d'Inverno*. Milano 1991

1992
ASCHENGREEN PIACENTI K., *Itinerario Laurenziano nel Museo degli Argenti*, Firenze
ASCHENGREEN PIACENTI K., *Quattro secoli di oreficeria al Museo degli Argenti*, in "Ori e tesori d'Europa", Atti del Convegno di Studi, Udine, pp. 71-78
COLLE E., *Palazzo Pitti. Il Quartiere del principe di Napoli*, Firenze
MASSINELLI A.M. - TUENA F., *Il Tesoro dei Medici*, Milano

1993
Una reggia per tre dinastie, Firenze

CONTENTS